THE ANGEL IN M

S0-AFF-823

Sukey Forbes is founder and president of an art, antiques, and interior design company and a blogger for *The Huffington Post*. She lives with her family near Boston.

Praise for *The Angel in My Pocket*

"A powerful, uplifting, and fearless look at what happens to a mother when a child dies suddenly, written without self-pity. . . . To walk along with Forbes—through pain, denial, her past, psychics, support groups, tattoos, and transcendentalism—is strangely soul-soothing and ultimately heartening. You can, you see, survive. But getting there may take a while."
                                                                    —*Chicago Tribune*

"There is a unique and lovely energy underlying this book—one that stems from Forbes's extended meditation on where Charlotte lands after her death. . . . Forbes's achievement in this book is that her engagement with 'the other side' is thoughtful and, yes, persuasive. . . . The best memoirs depict the movement toward transformation, and Forbes has certainly changed by the end of her book. She has written a complex story of love and grief in which she comes to live with hope and faith."
                                                                    —*The Boston Globe*

"A Boston Brahmin who had it all chronicles her experiences dealing with the tragic death of her beloved young daughter. . . . It wasn't until she took a friend's advice to see a medium that she began to accept Charlotte's passing as a form of spiritual transition and understand the depth of her connection to the Emersonian part of her heritage."
                                                                    —*Kirkus Reviews*

"What do we do when the unthinkable happens? We have choices, of course. We can break, become tough, allow cynicism to seep into all our broken places. Or, as Sukey Forbes illustrates in this remarkable book, grief can kick the door wide open and let the light in. *The Angel in My Pocket* is a devastating and beautiful paean to the human spirit."

—Dani Shapiro, author of *Still Writing*

"How do we bear the unbearable? In this heartbreaking book, a bereaved mother offers an unflinching account of the different ways we grieve and the different—and surprising—ways we may begin to heal."

—George Howe Colt, author of *The Big House*

"I was raised in the Boston area and this book brought back memories of my childhood. I loved the line in *The Angel in My Pocket* that says 'how important it is to let all the unimportant stuff go.'"

—Temple Grandin, author of *Thinking in Pictures*

"If your life has ever come to a halt, if you have wondered how to want to live again, if you are looking for hope and longing for courage in the face of grief, if you seek staunch honesty and are keen to hear it from someone who knows firsthand that privilege does not protect you from pain, read this book and know that you are not alone."

—Laura Munson, author of *This Is Not the Story You Think It Is*

"*The Angel in My Pocket* is one mother's response to that most visceral question that haunts the bereaved: Where has she *gone*? With spiritual curiosity and tenacious love, Sukey charts a heartfelt journey that grants grief its peaceful landing on a far shore."

—Nichole Bernier, author of *The Unfinished Work of Elizabeth D.*

Sukey Forbes

The Angel in My Pocket

A Story of Love, Loss, and
Life After Death

PENGUIN BOOKS

For Maraia,
so lovely to reconnect
with you.
← love →
Sukey Forbes

PENGUIN BOOKS
Published by the Penguin Group
Penguin Group (USA) LLC
375 Hudson Street
New York, New York 10014

USA | Canada | UK | Ireland | Australia | New Zealand | India | South Africa | China
penguin.com
A Penguin Random House Company

First published in the United States of America by Viking Penguin,
a member of Penguin Group (USA) LLC, 2014
Published in Penguin Books 2015

Photograph credits
Pages 32 and 120: Kersti Malvre
Other photographs courtesy of the author

THE LIBRARY OF CONGRESS HAS CATALOGED THE HARDCOVER EDITION AS FOLLOWS:
Forbes, Sukey.
The angel in my pocket : a story of love, loss, and life after death / Sukey Forbes.
pages cm
ISBN 978-0-670-02631-9 (hc.)
ISBN 978-0-14-312757-4 (pbk.)
1. Spiritualism—United States. 2. Forbes, Sukey. 3. Forbes, Charlotte,
1997–2004. 4. Children—Death. 5. Genetic disorders in children—Patients—Family
relationships—United States. 6. Consolation. 7. Ghosts—Massachusetts—Naushon
Island. 8. Naushon Island (Mass.) —Description and travel. I. Title.
BF1261.2.F67 2014
133.109744'92—dc23
2013047850

Printed in the United States of America
1 3 5 7 9 10 8 6 4 2

Set in Perpetua Std
Designed by Francesca Belanger

*Penguin is committed to publishing works of quality and integrity.
In that spirit, we are proud to offer this book to our readers;
however, the story, the experiences, and the words
are the author's alone.*

For Boo Bear, Sweetie Pea, and Beetle Bug

Contents

The Angel in My Pocket

1

Haunted

Just across the meadow from Mansion House on Naushon Island, there's a barn devoted entirely to genealogy. This newly renovated space, bright and spare as a Chelsea art gallery, serves as an archive for the eight generations of Forbeses who have summered here. Ancient maps depict the Elizabeth Islands, the tiny archipelago to which Naushon belongs, and which juts southwest from the underbelly of Cape Cod. Alongside the maps hang old sepia photographs and, as if we family members were racehorses, color-coded bloodlines. Each of us has his or her own card, and the cards are connected by differently colored ribbons. Each color represents a separate line of descent from John Murray Forbes, the young merchant in the China trade who in 1842 bought the entire six-thousand-acre preserve. Nine years earlier he had married Sarah Hathaway, with whom he had seven children. My particular line, marked by a blue ribbon, descends from William Hathaway Forbes, the eldest son, who shifted the family's enterprises from tea and opium and railroads to telephones. It proved to be a good decision.

From the time my own children could walk I've taken them to the barn at least once each year because I've always wanted to make them feel a part of this tradition. As they grew older, I tried to explain to them exactly what a "cousin" was, and what having an "uncle" meant, and how far back a "great-great-grandmother" reached in time, and what it meant to have a relative "once removed." I thought it was important for them to understand this larger backdrop to their lives, and for me to be able to say, "See. There *you* are. You belong. You're part of the clan." A quick glance around the room is all it takes to spy the recent births, marriages, divorces, and deaths. Each is highlighted by the temporary addition of a round colored sticker on the card.

I have three children, though only two of them are still with me physically. The card on the wall representing Charlotte, my middle child, has a red dot in the corner, and the dates December 23, 1997–August 18, 2004.

Whenever I visit the barn now I can still feel six-year-old Charlotte tugging on my shirt, trying to hurry me along, saying, "Come on, Mummy. I want to see *my* tag."

Charlotte's hair was a soft corn silk blond with red highlights, very straight and very shiny, and every time I was with her I wanted to touch it. She had freckles across the bridge of her nose, and a crooked little grin, and her eyes were large and green like her father's, with exceptionally long lashes. When I think of those eyes I remember how they were always opened wide and absorbing everything, almost as if she knew she did not have much time and she wanted to make the most of it.

I can still hear her commentary on what our ancestors wore in those old photographs, and how it was different from what she was wearing. Charlotte's fashion sense seemed to have emerged with her from the womb. Once, when I was still nursing her, I was in a meeting choosing fabrics for a project and this infant attached to my breast reached out a tiny hand and started stroking one of the bolts of cloth. Typically, the fabric that attracted Charlotte's attention was the one we ultimately went with for the sofa.

Charlotte was a girl's girl who loved to twirl and dance in fabulous fabrics, and after she began to dress herself she was known to wear one pink loafer and one blue one, which usually inspired me to do the same. Whenever she stole into my closet for dress-up, invariably she pulled out only the best cashmere sweaters. She also went straight for the Manolo Blahnik heels. When I hid them she'd come find me, tug on my sleeve, and say "Manolo." It was one of her first words.

And yet Charlotte was just as much a nature child, someone who fundamentally "got" Naushon. She loved to run through the fields and see shapes in the clouds and catch snakes and turtles out by the lake. But she also loved princesses, and as she began to learn to read and write, most of the stories she composed were about her own variations on Snow White and Cinderella. I remember her, just days before she died, dancing through a neighbor's garden, hopping about to taste each and every variety of arugula. I also remember her during berry-picking season. She'd just come back from a birthday party and was purple all over from making jam in the kitchen, but on top of the berry stains her face was painted like a tiger's.

A fairy princess and a critter catcher. A tiger who made jam. A middle child who nonetheless ruled the roost. The mystery that haunted me during my first months without her was: What happened to all these contradictions? All this exuberance? What about all this joy? They say my daughter died, but where exactly did my daughter go?

For me, the place for probing such questions has never been a grand cathedral, or an ashram, or even one of those stark white buildings beneath the steeple in the center of a New England village. The woods and meadows of Naushon have always been my church. And long before I knew anything about my great-great-great-grandfather, the poet Ralph Waldo Emerson, and how he helped develop such ideas into the school of thought called Transcendentalism, my approach to finding God was through the direct experience of nature.

I loved Naushon's forests and meadows because this was the one setting in which Forbes children were allowed to be rambunctious and expressive, even rapturous. For as long as I can remember we rode horses there and we sheared sheep. We drove pony carts, cleared trails with chain saws, put on plays in the forests, skinny-dipped on the beaches, rolled down the hills, and sang at the top of our lungs while tramping along the dirt roads. It was—and remains—a matter of pride among us to never use a flashlight when out walking at night, not even in the woods. If you're a Forbes, you're supposed to know the trails well enough that you can sense where you are.

This barefoot, unbuttoned life on Naushon was all the more precious because of the way it contrasted with the puritanical constraints imposed in all other respects by old-line families like the Forbeses—and there was no lightening up on my mother's side, either. The maternal genealogy reads like a "You Are Here" map at a New England prep school. Saltonstall, Cabot, Palfrey, Winthrop—the names above the entrances to the ivy-covered buildings are my family names.

For kids like us, brought up on formal teas and white-gloved dancing lessons, the wildness of Naushon provided the kind of soul nurturing that Brahmin propriety and reserve seemed to neglect. In me, its elemental beauty also inspired some very un-Brahmin soul searching, begun when I was young but brought to a crisis by my daughter's death.

To the extent that Naushon could never adequately answer my deepest questions about Charlotte, it could at least make me feel

Mansion House etching, 1856.

that, wherever she had gone, it was not so very far. Naushon had a way of uniting not only past and present, the spirit world and the natural world, but the living and the dead.

In the attic of Mansion House, built in 1809, the faces of long-dead ancestors are preserved in a series of plaster "death masks," which I remember from my childhood as fondly as some other girl might remember a gilt mirror from her mother's dressing table. And the collection is not nearly so morbid as it might seem—and often does seem to visitors who are brave enough to follow me up the rickety stairs and brush away the dust to see them. Using wax or plaster molds to preserve an image of the dead is a custom that goes well back into the Middle Ages and was still common at the end of the nineteenth century. These casts were often used in funeral ceremonies, as models for subsequent sculpting or engraving, and, before the advent of photography, for purposes of forensic identification. In Egypt, of course, there was a much more ancient tradition of stylized masks, made of gold, which were thought to guard the soul from evil spirits on its way to the afterlife.

On Naushon we didn't talk about life after death, or about the existence of a spirit world, and yet the references were all around us. Some of my ancestors are buried in a beech forest near the center of the island. Others gaze down from the oil paintings that line the entryway to Mansion House, and, yes, some of these paintings have eyes that seem to follow you around the room. Since 1855 there's been a sundial out front that carries this inscription:

> With warning hand I mark Time's rapid flight;
> From Life's glad morning to its solemn night,
> Yet through the dear God's love I also show
> There's a flight above me by the shade below.

It's hard to deny that the place carries a haunted-house vibe, with a soupçon of Miss Havisham and more than a hint of Peabody Essex Museum. In the Chestnut Parlor, elk antlers rest on top of the grand piano. Glass cases contain relics from the days of Hong Kong and clipper ships and the family's early investment in railroads, the telegraph, and the telephone. We have trinkets left by summer guests who included Daniel Webster, Herman Melville, Oliver Wendell Holmes, Generals Sheridan and Pershing, and U.S. presidents from Grant to Clinton. John Singer Sargent signed the leather-bound guest book when he came to paint portraits of the children, as did Frederick Law Olmsted when he dropped by to help with the gardens.

In the summer of 1811, James Bowdoin III, the man who built the big house and was its first resident, died so suddenly and mysteriously that family, servants, and farmhands all fled, leaving food on the table and in the cupboards. No one came back for seven years.

John Murray Forbes, the family patriarch, gives this account in his privately published *Reminiscences*:

Mr. James Bowdoin died very suddenly in the north-west upper room, and in the old armchair still kept there. His departure was so sudden that it was thought necessary to remove his remains at once to Boston, closing the doors of the Mansion House and merely turning the key, without clearing the dinner table or otherwise making the rooms habitable; and this is said to have remained exactly the situation here for about seven years. Somehow the story got around that Mr. Bowdoin had ordered this to be done, in the expectation of coming back at the end of seven years. However this may be so, the rumor of his haunting the house grew up. During all the years up to the building of the tower in 1881, I remember the old house as a very open one, not only to friends and shipwrecked guests, but also to wind and rain. All the windows were loose, all the shutters slammed and rattled, as did the doors; and the latches wearing loose permitted the doors, (especially that of the north-west room) to open of a windy night most uncannily. The cellar walls were not chinked up, the floor not plastered below; and, when the wind blew from the north, I have seen the parlor carpet rise up six to twelve inches, lifting with it a common chair . . .

When Secretary Stanton [Edwin Stanton, President Lincoln's secretary of war] visited us just after the war, he was much over-strained by the excitement of his long service, and a good subject for nerves. He was put into the haunted room, but nothing was said to him, as far as we could find out, about the ghost, and he left us without a word on that tender subject; but about two years ago a friend of his told me that Stanton had confided to him that he had here come nearer the supernatural than ever before.

Many years later, when my mother came for her first visit, she and my father were sitting on the porch and she was so uncomfortable that she had to keep moving around. After they'd gone inside, my father calmly informed her that the ghost of Mr. Bowdoin had been standing behind them the whole time.

The disembodied spirits of deceased family members were said to linger in the hallways, to haunt the bedchambers, and sometimes to join us for dinner. One autumn I received a thank-you note from a cousin who had hosted a large dinner party in our dining room. With it she included two photographs taken while they had all gathered around after dinner to sing at the far end of the table. Very clearly in the middle of the photograph is the white silhouette of a woman seated in profile wearing a shawl over her shoulders and her hair in a topknot. Grandmother Edith had clearly enjoyed the madrigals and seated herself at the head of the table to enjoy them. My cousin thought I would be pleased to have the photograph of her for the guest books.

I'd always accepted the presence of ghosts, as well as my

A ghostly silhouette appears at the head of the table in Mansion House, 2008.

family's very matter-of-fact acceptance of ghosts . . . matter-of-factly. But "ghosts" are as common as mice in creaky old New England houses. Was the idea of ghosts on Naushon just a game, or was there more to it? The question never came up. Then again, I knew the visceral experience. I work at an elaborately carved wooden partner's desk that was given as a gift to my great-great-uncle from Chiang Kai-shek when he was ambassador to Japan in the 1930s. Often when I sit down to work or to write I will smell cigarette smoke. I have come to consider this smoke as some familial entity who comes to inspire me in my work. I refer to this entity as my smoking muse. My smoking muse arrived with the desk. There is no explanation for its presence and I have just come to accept it and actually smile when it appears.

Great-great-great-grandfathers Ralph
Waldo Emerson and John Murray
Forbes with their first grandchild,
my great-grandfather Ralph Emerson
Forbes, 1868.

While my great-great-great-grandfather may have been the progenitor of Transcendentalism, much of the family moved well beyond him on the spectrum of unconventional beliefs, far more pagan than Puritan. And Naushon has always attracted more than its share of spiritual seekers, extending from Emerson himself (known locally as Grandpa Moo Moo) to Aldous Huxley—author of *Brave New World* and *The Doors of Perception*, popularizer of Vedanta, mescaline, and LSD.

For 150 years, our "blue" Forbes-Emerson descendants have embraced all manner of spiritual alternatives, ranging from Theosophy to Krishnamurti to mathematical astrology and the attempt to communicate with extraterrestrial beings. Over the decades, one family member or another has always kept the "doors of perception" wide open, sometimes banging in the breeze.

It's also true that, whether the product of emotional constraint, inbreeding, or simply the luck of the draw, the Forbes clan has always exhibited more than its share of garden-variety madness. There was John Murray Forbes's daughter Ellen, who flung herself into a gorge when her parents would not let her marry a man they deemed "inappropriate." Her mother had written to Ellen's brother William, saying, "I fear she has these bouts of insanity, and very likely you are going to wind up with an angel sister, and we an angel daughter."

And then there was my grandmother Irene, who spent much of her life in McLean Hospital, where she was often subjected to shock treatments. Her mental illness aside, I always thought she was exotic and glamorous. After all, she wore nail polish and cared about the way she looked. She had an apartment in Boston with modern furniture, and she was also a fallen women. She had been married to an Emerson (a different branch from the poet) before my grandfather David Cabot Forbes stole her away from him. (The frequent crossovers and overlaps are why we winkingly refer to Forbes genealogy as a family wreath rather than a family tree.)

Ralph W. Emerson's wife Lidian had visions, was said to be clairvoyant, and after the loss of their beloved son Waldo at age six, became a follower of Swedenborg, spent much of her life in bed, and became addicted to morphine. Emerson himself may have been the patriarch of a distinctly American voice in literature, but beneath the high collar and the frock coat, he was much more strangely mystical than the English professors let on. A year after the death of his first, very young wife, Ellen Louisa Tucker, he went to her crypt and opened it. "I just had to see," he wrote. He followed the same procedure after Waldo's death, gazing at his son's corpse "as if he was taking a long long look into eternity."

Lidian Emerson.

I had always struggled with my famous forebear's philosophy, finding it opaque, when deep down I wanted it to be as if I were sitting beside his chair and simply absorbing his wisdom, as if something in the DNA provided for a natural and easy transmission of his ideas. But the "transparent eyeball"? The "Oversoul"? It took me forever to realize that a schoolgirl appreciation and being able to fill in the right jargon on a quiz was not the point, and that the only thing that mattered about my famous ancestor's ideas was their resonance in the heart, not the head. There was a far more intuitive way of appreciating Emerson, along with everything else in the world, and that way was my way.

My first memory of a spirit encounter was very Emersonian in its merger of the natural and the supernatural, the domestic and demonic, and of course it took place on Naushon. We were staying in the big Stone House up on the hill above the harbor, my brother Jamie and I sharing a room, and there was a huge thunderstorm. I remember hollering until my mother finally relented and came in and got us. I had been terrified, and suddenly it turned very cozy. My father was smoking a pipe, standing in profile in front of a huge bay window that looked out over the harbor pasture, when lightning struck an old pump house and danced along the ground. I could have sworn I saw a human form emerge from that flash of electricity and walk across the field.

Given this family tradition of seeking and seekers, perhaps it was not so unusual that six months after Charlotte's death, when a friend suggested I might want to pay a visit to a medium—a woman with special abilities who was able to contact what's often called the Other Side—I was guarded, but not entirely resistant. In fact, this experience wound up changing my view of life, death—everything—fundamentally. It altered the course of my grieving to help me move away from mere suffering and complete the circle of my own personal search.

"In Nature every moment is new," Emerson wrote. "The past is always swallowed and forgotten; the coming only is sacred. Nothing is secure but life, transition, the energizing spirit . . . People wish to be settled; only as far as they are unsettled is there any hope for them."

2

Storm Warning

At Naushon, I'd always felt sheltered, grounded, and safe. The landscape of the Outer Banks, the cherished family spot of the very different tribe I'd married into, could not have been more different. When my husband, Michael, and I first began to vacation there, on what was not much more than a sandbar that ran just offshore and parallel to the North Carolina mainland for about seventy miles, I felt exposed and vulnerable.

For three summers we rented a place in Avon, a tiny town reachable only after a long, monotonous drive along a narrow road lined with pampas grass, windswept strip malls, sand-filled parking lots, and shingled houses that faced either the ocean or the bay. My first impression of that narrow spit of land must have come from sailors in my family telling stories of storms and shipwrecks, because I kept thinking about ghost ships and death by water. And about Roanoke, Virginia, the English colony just across the bay where, in the late 1500s, all the settlers disappeared without a trace.

We were living on the West Coast at the time. I'd been something of a rebel child, trying to escape the emotional straitjacket of my upbringing by relocating to California after college, and then, marriage and family life kept me there. But Michael and I relished the idea of East Coast vacations to keep us in touch with family. Naushon was the meeting place for the Forbes clan, and it was important to me that my children be a part of that. For my husband's large Irish family, the Bighams, the Outer Banks was just as sacred.

Some people loved being able to see water on either side, but I found the lack of trees and solid, higher ground disconcerting. There was something so tentative about those houses up on stilts, exposed to the wind and the open sea. I guess I was used to having more to hang on to. I needed less of a sense that everything around me had been put together last week, and that it could all be gone with the next high tide. I was a bit spooked, too, because just before our visit I had had a terrifying dream, of being on the Naushon ferry, of the children and I falling off. In my dream, I grabbed Cabot and Beatrice but I could not reach Charlotte, who slipped beyond my grasp into the sea. I woke up gasping, with the sickening feeling of having let my daughter drown yet knowing I could not save her.

If I found any reassurance during those two-week mini-reunions in North Carolina, it was in the presence of Annie, my sister-in-law. The wife of my husband's brother Harry, Annie was fun to spend time with, and a great mom, but she was also a pediatric anesthesiologist at a major teaching hospital. Avon was at least an hour from the nearest emergency room, but with Annie on the scene, at least I knew we were in good hands should one of the kids need medical attention.

Harry is a doctor, too, a cardiologist, but his patients tend to be on Medicare. Annie works with children, and beyond that, she's a force of nature, so much so that her nickname as a chief resident had been "Commando Anne." Her legend increased within the family when she performed successful abdominal surgery (general anesthesia, halothane in a mason jar) on Mr. Quiggles, her daughters' pet mouse.

Back when her girls were small, I used to rib Annie about the way she kept everything in her home locked down with child-proof latches, including the toilet seats—very problematic during personal urgencies in the middle of the night. Everywhere she went she carried a full emergency kit, including the bags and tubes for pediatric IV. I would venture to say we were the only vacationers on the Outer Banks equipped with airway kits and resuscitation masks in all sizes from infant to adult.

Getting from our home near San Francisco to the rental in North Carolina was a full day's travel no matter how we did it. The last time we made the trip, Cabot was five, Beatrice was eighteen months, and Charlotte was four—three little blond dervishes running through airports. All of us have fair skin, and standing in line, I often felt very aware of just how much we did not look like a study in American diversity. Sometimes I wondered if we were tempting fate by being too white, too privileged, too prosperous, or too happy. But that would change soon enough.

Our condo in Avon was right next door to Harry and Anne's, on the bay side, in a cul-de-sac with eight other identically shingled houses up on stilts. Harry and Michael's parents were there as well, and they shared our unit with us. It was one big, happy family with no pretentions, no privacy, and no lock-jawed WASP emotional reserve.

The North Carolina coast can get stinking, steamy hot in August, and as a result, much of our vacation life took place on one of the large porches that each of the houses had on the second floor. The children could be contained, playing safely, while the breeze kept everyone cool. We would lounge out there, shifting from coffee and tea and newspapers to books and board games, followed by a snooze, followed by cocktails and dinner.

The complex also had a swimming pool, and Charlotte in particular loved to escape the heat by splashing in the water. She used to say to me, "Mummy, I like to be fresh and cool." Anne and Harry's girls, Grace and Julie, were eight and ten that summer, and they made a wonderful fuss over their four-year-old cousin, treating Charlotte like a little princess, playing endless games of Marco Polo under the watchful eye of various parents, as well as Grandmom and PopPop Bigham.

At the end of one perfectly ordinary day, we gathered at Anne and Harry's for dinner, and any meal that I don't have to manage is a perfect meal in my book. The kitchen gene simply did not express itself in me, and I've always been happy to defer to someone else's expertise, especially when it's a take-charge personality like Anne's.

The conversation around the table was highly animated, as it always was in the Bigham family, and after a little wine had been shared it took serious effort to capture the floor and work in your particular anecdote. The Bighams have never been afraid to embellish whenever a few frills might be required to top what had already been a tall tale. Coming from my rather austere New England background, I loved all this emotional energy, the way the whole family would lean in and listen when Harry Senior went on about his grandmother delivering moonshine during the Depression, or his own experiences as a GI in Italy at the end of World War II. The kids especially hung on his every word.

After dinner we piled into the cars and drove off to get ice cream cones, which was a ritual rated just below Communion in the Bighams' spiritual universe. Our group of eleven overwhelmed the small ice cream parlor, but after a while everyone had his or her favorite flavor. Then, with cones in hand, we moved outside to the lawn and watched the late setting sun glide down into the bay. We have photographs of the children with ice cream on their faces, turning cartwheels and playing in the fading light of that hot and sticky summer evening.

Getting the kids to bed that night was easy. When they were small I used to sing a John Denver song to them called "For Baby," which begins, "I'll walk in the rain by your side." When I got to the line in the chorus that says, "And the wind will whisper your name to me," I'd lean down and whisper "Cabot" and "Charlotte." (Beatrice, still too young for this sort of thing, was already asleep in her own little room.) I finished the song, gave each of the kids a kiss, and tiptoed out. Charlotte and Cabot were both asleep before I reached the bedroom door.

It was about an hour later when I heard the scream. There was such an urgency mixed with terror in that voice that it haunts me to this day. I ran to the children's room and saw Charlotte sitting up in her bed. I went to her and pulled her close, but her head against my chest was so hot I felt scalded.

I called out to Michael. "Charlotte's sick. Come help me."

Then I picked her up and carried her into the bathroom. I put her in the tub, turned on the faucet, and began splashing cold water over her. Charlotte had never really had any serious issues. Certainly she'd never had a fever like this.

Michael came in and hovered over my shoulder. "What is this? What's happening?"

Charlotte had begun to point her toes, her feet curling inward. This was very weird, and made me very worried. I tried to stay in the moment, not letting my imagination run away to all the awful places it could go.

"How do you feel, Sweet Pea?" I asked her.

She stared up at me but didn't speak. She was conscious—she was not having a seizure—but I didn't know what the hell was going on. The muscle in her jaw began to twitch. Then I watched as her calf muscles contracted, then her thigh muscles, then her torso and her arms.

"I'm getting Anne and Harry," Michael said. And then he was gone. I waited, feeling sick to my stomach as I watched my daughter locked in these painful contortions.

A few moments later the two doctors appeared in the bathroom, Annie with her black bag, their two girls trailing behind and looking very tentative. Within a couple of minutes Annie had sized up the situation, hung an IV bag from the shower rod, and had a line carrying fluids into a vein in the crook of Charlotte's arm. My daughter was still frighteningly rigid, but the worst of it was that she couldn't control her neck. We were all on her left, but her head was turned to the right, her eyes focused on the wall.

I glanced up just long enough to catch the eye contact between Anne and Harry. The level of concern that registered on their faces was not what I wanted to see. But at least they were with us. At least we were not stuck on this sandbar in the middle of nowhere with all the medical expertise of an MBA and an art history major.

Annie sent the girls to get all the ice out of the refrigerators. When little Julie came back with the first bucket, Anne dumped it into the bathwater. Charlotte was throwing off so much heat that the ice turned to liquid as soon as it hit the surface. Grace came in with a second bucket from the condo next door, and Anne poured that in as well. It also melted instantly.

For a moment we stared at the water and held our collective breath. That was all the ice we had. We were going to need more ice.

Harry used a digital thermometer to take Charlotte's temperature. The device began to beep at 105—as high as it would go.

"Should we call an ambulance?" I asked.

I expected these two very competent doctors to say, "No need. Got it covered."

But without missing a beat, both of them gave me an emphatic yes.

We had to wait a very long while for the EMTs, and while we waited my heartbeat was so loud I was sure everyone else could hear it. The gnawing in my stomach got worse and worse, but then the situation improved. The fluids transfusing into Charlotte's veins and the cooling water surrounding her seemed to be bringing her fever down. Her rigidity began to soften, and she could even turn her head to look at me. But Anne and Harry still had these grave expressions, and they were still carrying on their own private doctor conversation with their eyes.

After what seemed like forever, the emergency team arrived and we briefed them on the situation. They lifted Charlotte onto the stretcher and got her ready for transport forty-five miles north to the hospital in Nags Head.

Anne and Harry said they would stay behind with Cabot and Beatrice. The grandparents were rather miraculously still asleep in another part of the house.

I would have preferred for our in-house physicians to go with us, because I trusted them a lot more than I trusted those EMTs. The only thing I said, though, was that I was going to ride with Charlotte. Michael got in the car behind us and we set off.

This was the first time I'd ever envied my husband his Catholicism. I wanted to pray, but I didn't really know how. Instead, my mind filled with all the negative possibilities, all the existential horrors that I knew were out there like the blank landscape and the night sky and the equally empty waters of the bay.

Later, Michael would tell me that he spent the entire drive trying to work out a deal. His job is all about negotiation, and he begged God not to take Charlotte, at least not that night. We both knew that small, innocent children die every day, but Michael made the case that, even from an entirely selfish perspective, there just ought to be some recognition for all the years of devotion he'd put in, all the times he'd said the Lord's Prayer and the Hail Mary. God had to do what God had to do—just not now, please.

We passed along the darkened road lined with pampas grass, the windswept strip malls, the sand-filled parking lots, and after a while Charlotte seemed better, cooler, and she began to chat with me. We both were still terrified, but we settled into the standard routine of "mother sits at sick child's bedside and works to distract, amuse, and comfort." I sang songs to her, and we talked about all the ordinary, fun things that had happened that day. I tried to acknowledge the fear she obviously was experiencing, while also trying to lessen her fear by dismissing the gravity of the situation. If only I could reassure myself.

Michael, of course, was not in on any of this. When he pulled up to the emergency entrance behind the ambulance, he did not know whether his child would be dead or alive. I watched him step out of the car and almost swoon when he saw me smiling.

"Hey, Sweetie Pea!" he called out to Charlotte. I'd never seen him look so vulnerable.

I watched the tension in his body fall away as she said, "Hi,

Daddy!" His prayers had been answered. God was on our side. At least for now.

The ER docs were able to see us right away. They made Charlotte comfortable and monitored her vital signs as her fever continued down into the normal range. She had a bad bout of diarrhea, but she appeared to have stabilized.

"A nasty rotavirus," they said, combined with dehydration. But somehow I knew that wasn't the case. As much as I wanted to believe it, something in my gut told me that we weren't going to get off so lightly.

But the doctors smiled reassuringly, wished us a good night, and sent us home.

Michael and I rode back to Avon in stunned silence, staring out at that isolated beach road once again, with Charlotte asleep in the backseat. I looked out into the blankness of the dark ocean surrounding us and, in my head, kept hearing a Gordon Lightfoot lyric that asks about the love of God and where it goes when it disappears. It was from a song about a shipwreck.

My sister Laura had seen that dark side. Her son Dawson, the same age as Cabot, had been diagnosed with acute lymphocytic leukemia at the age of four. For the first time it hit me that I never really understood what she'd been going through. How can you understand, unless you have a child in that kind of situation yourself? The Greeks said that we suffer into wisdom. I didn't want to gain that kind of understanding. I wanted Charlotte to be well.

When we got to the condo I reported in to Anne and Harry while Michael carried Charlotte up to bed. When Michael came back down to talk, he related a version of our experience at the hospital that was more upbeat than mine. He seemed to accept the

ER physicians' assessment at face value. Neither Anne nor Harry said anything, but I saw a glance pass between them. They gave us hugs and their own reassurances, and after they left, Charlotte slept through until morning. Neither of her parents slept a wink.

The sun came up and it was sweltering as usual. We turned the air-conditioning to high and kept Charlotte inside. Generally she seemed fine, but she was so sore from the muscle contractions of the night before that she hobbled around as if she'd just run a marathon. At breakfast, to cheer her up, Michael told her that she walked like the most adorable little penguin he'd ever seen.

I assumed that if I could just stop shaking and start breathing again, maybe we could get back to having a vacation while we were still on vacation. We'd dodged a bullet, and now I wanted to put it all behind us.

Around midmorning I saw Annie out on the lawn in front of their house. She was wearing a black Speedo, playing with the children, drinking her coffee, and helping Harry tack up a windsurfer for his first sail of the day.

I pulled on a pair of shorts and a T-shirt, grabbed a cup of tea, and walked downstairs. The kids had caught a fish and were giggling and chatting as they watched it swim around in a bright red bucket.

I walked across the lawn and gave my sister-in-law a big hug. "Annie, we can't thank you enough for last night." Even as the words came out of my mouth they seemed so inadequate, pathetic. But it was her response that set me back on my heels.

She took a sip of her coffee and glanced over at Harry.

"Sukey, we were lucky last night. That could have ended very differently."

I felt as if I'd been kicked in the gut. She looked so grim. I was actually a little ticked off at her for reverting so quickly to "Commando" mode. Why did she always have to find the cloud in front of every silver lining?

Anne was silent for a moment, and I could tell she was trying to decide how to say something she knew I would not want to hear. When she turned to me, it was with a focus more intense than I'd ever seen from her before.

"Sukey, I want you to listen to me very carefully," she said. This was the chief of pediatric anesthesia speaking, not just my sister-in-law, and her eyes were burning into mine. "Last night was one of the scariest moments of my entire career."

My hand went limp, nearly pouring tea down my legs.

"There's a condition called malignant hyperthermia," she went on. "It's genetic. It's so rare that the average pediatrician will never see it. I'm an anesthesiologist in a teaching hospital, so I've seen it a lot."

I took a deep breath to try to slow my pulse. "You're saying there's more to what happened last night than what happened last night? Like another shoe that could drop."

"That's exactly what I'm saying."

I looked out across the bay, and the sweat in my scalp began to bead up. I saw all that open water and felt the heat and then the sense of emptiness and vulnerability swept over me again. Annie's assessment made perfect sense. I felt the truth of it in my bones— I just didn't want to acknowledge it. Ostrich style, if we never admitted the danger, then maybe it would just go away.

"We see it in the OR all the time," she went on. "The trigger's usually halothane or another agent we use, a muscle relaxant that's like curare. But there's also something called a nontriggered malignant hyperthermic reaction. I think that's what we saw with Charlotte last night."

Defended as I was against the message, I was also too afraid, and too limp in the heat, to resist it. So I just listened, staring blankly.

"Marines in boot camp, football players dropping dead in August . . . That's a heatstroke. This is different. This is in the cells of the skeletal muscles going completely haywire. That's why we saw the rigidity in Charlotte's limbs last night. All it takes is a touch of fever from a cold, the flu . . . anything. Hypermetabolism moves through the body like a wrecking crew. Potassium leaks out of the cells and into the pericardium and you go into cardiac arrest."

I'd heard more than I could absorb. I started scanning the bay again, wishing I could simply vanish into it.

Then she added, "By all rights and logic, Charlotte should have died."

For another moment I stood silent, feeling the hot wind scorch my face as Anne and I looked into each other's eyes.

"What should we do?" I said.

"There's an antidote called dantrolene. That's what you use when this happens in the OR. Every hospital keeps it on hand, but it's not foolproof. So the important thing is to never let it get that far."

"Which means . . ."

"It's imperative that you tell your pediatrician about this and have it entered into Charlotte's records."

I nodded, but I could just see our doctor rolling her eyes and writing me off. One more Internet Mom with too much time on her hands and too much half-baked information from a million crackpot Web sites.

I asked Anne if she would speak directly with Charlotte's doctor for me. She said that I should stick to my guns, but that, if need be, she would be willing to call her up as well.

But, owing to the nature of the disease, Anne and I talked about prevention, not cure.

"Outdoor sports in the heat," Anne said, "things like tennis and softball—out. Hot yoga—out."

"Are you sure? I mean, I know you know your stuff, but . . ."

"There's a diagnostic test, but it involves removing a square-inch chunk of tissue from the quadriceps muscle. If the muscle contracts in response to the reagent, the test is positive. Trouble is, the test doesn't get you anywhere because at the end of the day there's really nothing we can do to make this go away or even make it better. The best approach is simply to assume she has malignant hyperthermia and act accordingly. Manage her activities accordingly. Hope for the best."

"Hope for the best . . . ," I repeated.

After a while I said, "No test, then."

"After what I saw last night, there's really no doubt in my mind. I think we should just pretend she had the test and that it came back positive."

At dinner that night I thought I saw Anne watching Charlotte more intently than usual, her eyes softer than usual. At the time, I chalked it up to a new attachment based on getting through the crisis together. Looking back now, I interpret that look as Doctor Anne knowing what was ahead for my daughter, and feeling a special compassion.

Before we left North Carolina, Michael and I spoke to Annie again several times to make sure we knew everything that could be done and were set up to do it. Then I think Michael, ever the optimist, always trusting in God, filed the anxiety away. Me—I remained devastated and confused, but at least I had my marching orders. I always do best with marching orders. Manage her fevers. Hope for the best.

As soon as we got back to California I spoke to our pediatrician. I tried to explain that my sister-in-law was a specialist who saw this syndrome a lot, but, just as I'd expected, this Bay Area doctor looked at me like I was from Mars. Even with my most persistent nagging, it took three checkups before I succeeded in getting her to enter the suspicion of malignant hyperthermia into Charlotte's record. In the end, though, just as Annie had explained, there was really nothing more she or anyone else could do. We could monitor and maintain, but we could not cure.

Over the next two years, Michael and I followed every precaution, especially Annie's warning about no strenuous activities in the heat. Charlotte had the usual bouts with colds and flu, the usual fevers, and each time, following Annie's instructions, I managed the temps with alternating doses of Tylenol and Motrin to maximize the consistency and effectiveness. With time, though, it became easier to qualify those dire warnings with the fact that Commando Anne was prone to worst-case scenarios.

Increasingly, even as we continued to do all the right things and to follow all the necessary precautions, I let the specific threat fade deeper into my unconscious. Call it denial if you want, but it's also called not being able to get your head around the idea that your child has a time bomb inside her that no one knows how to dismantle.

When Charlotte died almost two years to the day after the incident on the Outer Banks, the pediatrician who had been dismissive of my concerns called me to offer condolences. I can't remember exactly what she said, but a large part of it had to do with feelings of guilt, a territory I would explore extensively over the years to come. I had been right, of course, but vindication was the last thing I wanted. I would give anything to have been wrong.

What that conversation did accomplish was to underscore the lesson that I should always trust my instincts, that statistics and rational deductions can take you only so far, and that much of our existence lies well to the margins of the bell curve. As my great-great-great-grandfather wrote a century and a half ago, "Sorrow makes us all children again—destroys all differences of intellect. The wisest knows nothing."

3

To Whom Much Is Given

From the window of the small seaplane I could see the familiar outline of Naushon, then Pasque, and then Nashawena, the last island in the archipelago before Cuttyhunk. Farther out, beyond Martha's Vineyard and Nantucket, the rising sun glinted off the blue Atlantic on a gorgeously clear summer morning.

It was just a short hop from the mainland, and soon we were descending over a red farmhouse beside a pond with swans gliding across the surface. From the green meadows above, Highland cattle were meandering down toward the bright, white beaches, and even though I'd seen these scenes a thousand times, I shook my head in disbelief at just how beautiful it was.

The pilot took us around again, and on the second pass I could see our cousins standing in the yard, looking up, pointing and waving. Then the blue of the pond again, the tall grass blowing, the snowy egrets rising out of the marsh, and I burst into tears. "Why are you crying?" my kids asked, and then I had to laugh. It wasn't only that these islands were so tear-inducingly beautiful. It was that I was just so very, very glad to be back. I'd been in California for fifteen very happy years, but as much as I'd loved it there, New England and Naushon had been calling me home.

Once there'd been a "kingdom by the sea," and therein a love so perfect that—at least according to Edgar Allan Poe—it inspired envy on the part of the angels, who Poe fingered for the death of his beautiful Annabel Lee. I never blamed God or the angels for what was about to happen to us, but I do remember this one moment of transcendent beauty as we soared above the islands, thinking that nobody had a right to be so incredibly lucky to have such a perfect family, and such a perfect place.

We did a water landing, then motored up to the dock where my cousin, her husband, and their two children were waiting. They gave us hugs, then helped us lug our stuff—mostly canvas bags loaded with windbreakers and many different colors of Crocs—from the plane to their small off-road vehicle.

My cousin's branch of the Forbes clan had bought Nashawena as an enterprise entirely separate from the family's ownership of Naushon. My cousin and I were exactly the same age, and we'd actually met as adults on the bigger, family island, only to discover that we were then living in the same town in California. The joke was that this was my first trip to her place, even though I'd summered a mile or two away my entire life.

But this was a year of major transitions when I was determined to break down all the old barriers and reconnect with what truly mattered. I wanted to slow it down, settle in, and extract every ounce of pleasure I could from this beautiful world that I was re-embracing as my birthright.

Happily, the kids were a great match from the get-go. Our Beatrice and their Rachel were both three. Alex and Charlotte were six, and Cabot, the senior man at seven, was highly adaptable, which meant that their mothers were able to slip away and go for long jogs all over the island, darting through the cattle as we cut across the meadows, occasionally being followed by a seemingly very curious coyote.

But most of the time both families huddled as one big group outside, enjoying the perfect weather. That first afternoon we had

Beatrice, Charlotte, and Cabot, summer 2004.

a picnic on the beach, and the kids played in a stream that emerged from one of the sand dunes. They caught crabs off the dock, then spent hours climbing around in a magnificent tree fort where several branches had grown together in a bog—all very *Swiss Family Robinson.*

Later, back at the house, after an outdoor shower and tick checks, we all waded through their meticulously maintained garden to gather vegetables for dinner. The sun was giving everything that honey-colored Kodachrome glow as the caretaker stood by to steer us off any produce that wasn't quite ready for picking.

The farmhouse on Nashawena had been built in 1820, and it had been left pretty much as it was. Captain Merrill had lived there for years and is known to roam the halls smoking his pipe. Many family members have smelled tobacco in the house even though no smoker has been in residence there for decades. There was no electricity—we ate by the light of oil lamps and candles—and there was a hand pump for water, and saggy beds and horsehair mattresses, but the grilled fish with vegetables less than an hour off the stem were incredible.

Around the table we played High Low, a game that Michael had invented as a way to get the kids to communicate. We went around the circle and everyone had to talk about the high point of their day, as well as the low. Oddly, they never got around to me, but I think I would have struggled to come up with anything I could have singled out that was less than perfect. I could now truthfully say that I had everything I wanted in life, made perfect by a magical new beginning, replete with new discoveries for my kids.

Just before bed we had the kids draw pictures and write notes for the fairies. We had a long-standing tradition of making up stories about fairies, and here the added touch was for the children to go out into the pasture at dusk and put the notes and drawings in the "fairy holes." Then, in the early morning sunlight, when the dew was sparkling on the "fairy blankets" of spiderwebs spread across the high grass, the kids would go out and, to their amazement, find gumdrops and little surprises in the places they had left notes. The fairies would keep the notes.

We'd moved back east in June and immediately put the kids in camp for a couple of weeks, hoping they'd have a chance to get to make some friends in their new town of Weston, in the Boston burbs. Then we'd spent the entire month of July on Naushon, making a major commitment to simplifying and circling the wagons. We limited the number of guests, and those who were invited came down just for the day rather than the week. I was focused on getting to know my extended family again. It was a time of quiet consolidation and built-in companionship. It was all about reconnecting with the long traditions that were my birthright. I'd grown up in Boston but I'd become an adult in California. In Boston I'd never felt the Sukey so much as the Forbes. In California I'd left the Forbes behind and let the Sukey emerge. Now I wanted to reconcile and integrate the two parts of my identity.

When I was younger, I'd often resented the fancy, dynastic hoo-ha I was supposedly a part of, so I came of age desperate to see what life was like where nobody really cared about crusty old New England bloodlines or even knew the names. I couldn't wait to get away from big, drafty houses, long on charm but short on heat, from the overcooked roast beef and soggy vegetables, from the requirement that we accomplish but never strive. So right out of college I moved to San Francisco, where Michael and I met and got married, and where, as Sukey Bigham, I gave birth to three children.

During our Wild West phase, Michael's very un-WASPy ambition made the most of the gold rush in biotech. He came out of the Stanford business school in 1983 and went to work in investment banking focused on health care. He became CFO, later COO, of a company that developed a highly successful AIDS drug and flu treatment. He took enormous risk professionally and it was a very wild but exhilarating ride. It went public in 1992, so when Michael left three years later it was on a healthy cushion of stock.

Just about everyone we knew in California was in a similar situation. They had houses that were plenty big, wiring that was up to code, and perfect climate control. The vegetables they served were crisp, the parties they gave were fabulous, and everybody was rolling in bright, shiny new money—a scene my grandmother would have dismissed with the withering arch of a single brow.

A leader in his field and at the top of his game, Michael joined a company developing monoclonal antibodies, which he ran for four years and then took public. After that, we decided to cash out and take a couple of years off to smell the roses, or at least the redwoods.

We moved from Silicon Valley up into the Santa Cruz Mountains on forty acres we bought that abutted another five hundred acres of timber that had been put into conservation. The property came with a Japanese Craftsman–inflected house with exposed beams, a caretaker cottage, a guesthouse, a boat-building studio, and a lumber mill. For three years we lived completely off the grid, like posh pioneers who could nonetheless jet away whenever we felt like it. Our friends were all self-selected rich people pretending to be rednecks, on the lam from Hollywood, Silicon Valley, or the wine business, and we thought we had it made.

We had propane for power and heat, and, in addition to our own well, riparian rights to the creek that flowed down the mountain (and supplied all of Santa Cruz). We pulled off water, but it had too much iron, so we treated it with reverse osmosis and ultraviolet light in our own water treatment plant with three twenty-thousand-gallon tanks. We also had a pond, fully lined and treated for swimming, and a waterfall. In keeping with our theme of self-reliance, we raised chickens in a wheeled cage that we made on site to the specifications of each of the planting beds. We could move the "chicken tractor" with the birds in it around our vegetable garden, letting the fertilizer fall like rain when the beds were fallow.

Every year we went to a "pick your own" farm in Santa Cruz and came back with buckets of olallieberries. This is when Charlotte and I would spend the rest of the day making jams and pies. She loved to be my helper on this, stirring the sugar into the pot, spooning the hot jam into the jars, then securing the lids and turning them over to cool. But she took even greater pride in writing "Bonny Doon Olallieberry Jam" on the labels in her own rather inventive script. We'd give the jam as gifts to our friends throughout the year, and when the supply started to run low she would start asking me how long until the next berry-picking season.

I loved the rustic life, but as the mother of three small children, I began to feel housebound and often isolated, so over time it became for me a little too rustic. It also cost a lot to live in Silicon Valley and in Santa Cruz, and so our kids rarely saw anyone who didn't have money. I began to wonder if raising the kids in such a rarefied environment, top-heavy with the "haves" and "have mores," was really such a great idea.

I loved the way the wind blew off the Pacific, the feel of it and the smell of it. We had a view of Monterey Bay, and the ocean was just a five-minute drive down the hill. There were the wild sweet peas and the very tall redwoods, and it was incredibly vast and beautiful and picturesque in the way that a national park would be all those things. But the Pacific is cold, the feel of the sand is heavy and grainy, and it was always a reminder to me that I wasn't home.

And yet I can remember sitting in the gazebo with the three kids nestled in under a blanket and waiting for the sound of

Michael's car coming up the hill from Highway 1 at twilight. We could hear him slow down or accelerate as he took each gentle twist and turn of the three-mile drive. The children were drifting off to sleep in my arms. I listened to the wind through the redwoods, and I remember thinking that the wind was whispering to me, "It just doesn't get any better than this."

Michael and I were standing in the dining room once, looking out the window over our garden and the redwoods and to the bay far beyond, and he said, "You know, we're going to look back on this as the happiest time in our lives." Six months later Charlotte was dead, and everything seemed smashed to hell.

I was dropping Cabot off at school one day when one of the fathers pulled in in a well-appointed pickup with blood dripping down out of the bed. He had just shot a couple of wild boars on the way in and I got this sudden rush of nostalgia, remembering how I would follow my father around during hunting season. One year he hacked off a turkey claw and gave it to me to take to show-and-tell. The next year it was an entire deer leg. My fellow classmates did not share my enthusiasm for this specimen, and I remember both times being sent home early from school with my burlap-and-twine-wrapped treasure in hand. Eventually my father taught me how to field dress a deer—the kind of thing that not all young ladies from fine old Boston families know how to do.

In that moment outside the school in Santa Cruz—after all that time away and all my complaints about needing to be "free to be me"—I realized just how much I missed the crusty old WASPs who were, after all, my mother and father, my aunts and uncles, my grandparents. Our trips home to Naushon had become increasingly wistful. "Too bad we can't come here year-round," we said to each other. And so we'd begun looking at real estate in Massachusetts.

Michael had been doing a little consulting and limited investing with venture capital firms in Silicon Valley, and when one of those outfits invited him to become a partner, he told them, "Well, we've been thinking of moving back east." They said, "Great. Open an office for us." So the idea of moving back east slipped into high gear.

We focused our real estate search in Concord, where my mother lived, but then someone said something about the Meadowbrook School in Weston. We took a look and we liked it, and then we happened to drive down Orchard Avenue and thought how much it seemed like a country lane in Vermont. We looked at the meadows on either side of the road and the huge oak trees and agreed that we'd move tomorrow if we could find a house right here. Then a home came up and we made the decision to buy it even before we stepped inside.

It was the caretaker cottage on three and a half acres of the old Hubbard estate. The house had a certain 1840s charm, but it had also been subjected to some horrendous renovations. We didn't really care, because what we really loved was the old blacksmith's forge with the bellows still in place that stood just a few feet away. Our idea was to live in the house for a couple of years, then knock it down and build a new place with the forge as the kitchen and family room.

We bought the property, and then I spent the next six months coming back on weekends to check in on the painting and the carpeting and other work we'd commissioned to make the place livable. That's when I discovered how incredibly welcoming the neighbors were. Everybody came by with a cake or cookies, and we especially loved our next-door neighbors, who were Livingston Taylor, the singer-songwriter, and his wife and manager, Maggie. We would always find her out wheeling a wheelbarrow around her garden, and she was very sweet with the children. I liked her immediately, but I think she was wary of me at first, seeing me as a bit too materialistic. She had a bumper sticker that read, "Want less." Looking back now, I see it as an omen, or perhaps a koan that encapsulated all the world's lessons about human vulnerability.

Our weekend visit with my cousin on Nashawena had been the briefest of interludes. Camp was still going on back in Weston, so on Monday morning, bright and early, the pilot was waiting at the dock with his seaplane to take us back to the mainland. Even as we left, though, we knew we'd be back. One of the reasons we'd chosen Weston was that it was hardly more than an hour from Woods Hole, the tiny town on Cape Cod where the ferries left for the islands. Weekends nestling back within the old enclave were going to be a regular part of our lives now.

On August 14 we came back to Naushon for Members Meeting. This is the annual family council for making big decisions about managing the property, but it's also a family reunion with big feasts and, WASPs being WASPs, lots of games.

Psychologists say that a joke can be an epitaph for an emotion. For New England clans like mine, competitive group activity and high jinks may be necessary as a way to fill the otherwise stony silence of emotional restraint.

On Naushon, the games include High Seas, a quintessentially Forbes activity invented by my great-great-uncle Cam, which is basically Capture the Flag on horseback. The playing field is an up-island square mile bisected by the main island road, but the action begins with each participant picking up a horse at the stables, then gathering at the sundial in front of Mansion House. There, everyone endures a ceremonial reading of the rules, despite the fact that anyone over the age of six knows them by heart. Certain players are designated "Merchants," and they have to take a playing card from their home port to their destination without being caught by the "Pirates." The Merchants have "Cruisers" who can accompany them, either as foils or spies. There are various jails and other significant landmarks, but you'll get caught in an instant if you rely on the main paths, so it pays to know the woods well enough that you can bushwhack and gallop back and forth. The horses love the competition and the excitement of the pack, and like some of the riders they get incredibly frothed up.

On this particular weekend, High Seas was followed by the

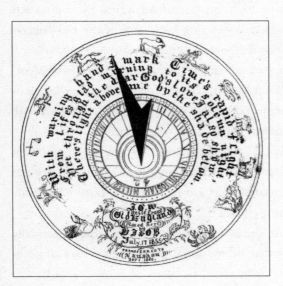

Etching of the old English sundial given as a gift to the family, with original verse composed for the dial by friend John Greenleaf Whittier in 1855.

Bennet Yacht Club regatta, named after John Murray Forbes's older brother Robert Bennet Forbes, a pioneering sea captain in the China trade. His hobby had been constructing scale models of sailing ships, which were given to the Forbes children and lovingly preserved. These are fully rigged schooners and sloops, three to four feet long, but the "Yacht Club" business is all very tongue-in-cheek. There's a commodore and a registered burgee, created in response to the fleet of New York Yacht Club boats that used to descend on our harbor every August, en masse, with passengers and crew then coming ashore for cocktails. This was back in the day when everyone who was anyone knew everyone else who was anyone. Now not so much.

The racecourse is in the outer harbor, where there is a prevailing southwest wind. It's one straight tack from the ledges to the Uncatena dock, so it's all about having the rudder and rigging set properly. There are different classes, a committee boat, trophies and medals—the whole nine yards. Observers go out in kayaks, Whalers, rowboats—whatever's available—to follow the competition, and the typical WASP refreshments of cheap lemonade and Oreo cookies are served throughout. Cocktails come afterward, followed by lots of jumping off the docks.

These silly summer pleasures were allowing me to renew the oldest roots and tendrils of my life. The time was packed with powerful, intensive memories of the way I used to live, and the promise of getting to live that way again. But more than that, it was the chance to see my children in this beloved and familiar context, absorbing their own rich sensory impressions, like the smell of Hudson Bay blankets that have been kept in storage too long, or the scanty portions of overcooked food, or the sound of ice tinkling in glasses filled with very good single-malt scotch

Island picnic, 1894.

Sheeping, circa 1960.

or cheap gin, both brought over in vast quantities. Wine was rarely served in my youth. Those who did not care for liquor drank sherry.

One of my most treasured childhood memories is of being on the island late in the season and using one of the frosted-glass half-gallon jugs that had been filled with water and warmed by the hearth to then warm the bed in my unheated room. Nine o'clock would have me climbing the stairs, not with a teddy bear but with a repurposed Gilbey's gin jug tucked under my arm.

WASPs are supposed to be God's frozen people, brought up close to our horses but at arm's length from our emotions. Sounds right to me.

We were a clan with a perverse sense of pride for mastering an austere life of deprivation despite multigenerational wealth, confirming our assumption of genetic superiority. A regal carriage with a swift gait gave the message of importance and quiet arrogance. Words were to be chosen wisely; one was meant to be able to defend one's opinion without raising one's voice. Anything that threatened the cool veneer—and that included being passionate or, God forbid, shedding tears for any reason—was seen as weakness. A cross word. Excitement over an upcoming trip or adventure. Anything that steered off the straight and narrow and gave insight into one's humanity was to be avoided at all costs. Not an unkind group but certainly more aloof than approachable. Manners, after all, were very important.

My grandfather David Cabot Forbes worked for the J. M. Forbes Company, which managed family investments. He was a lawyer, trained at Harvard, and he was also head trustee of Naushon. Apparently he did a fine job of it, because he was consulted by other

families with large land trusts—the Rockefellers, the Kennedys—
to see how we pulled it off.

My grandmother had serious emotional problems, which meant
that David's son, my father, Ralph Murray Forbes, was raised
mostly by his older sister and by his aunt, and his relationship with
his mother was more that of a caretaker. As a young man he would
receive calls from the manager of the Chilton Club in Boston.
"Please come pick up your mother. She's causing a ruckus." Eventually, my Forbes grandfather divorced my Forbes grandmother,
after which my grandmother took up with her chauffeur.

Ralph, my father, was named after his grandfather, who was
named after his grandfather, who was the famous Ralph Waldo.
With this treasured appellation allotted only once every other
generation, family expectations were high, and my father did his
part at Milton Academy, and then at Harvard, and then by becoming senior vice president of Bank of Boston. If the right look
and the right pedigree were all it took, then he was every bit the
young go-getter destined for great things. He was athletic, gifted,
and charming, the eldest son destined to take over the family
reins, including the Naushon Trustees.

And if the objective had been to create Boston society's Golden
Couple, then the perfect partner for Ralph Forbes was my mother,
Natalie Saltonstall. They had grown up in the same Brahmin circles. Their parents were friends—they had ski houses near each
other in New Hampshire, and my mother's family had visited
Naushon for generations as dear family friends. The Saltonstalls
had arrived in the New World via the Winthrop fleet in 1630 and,
aside from the Winthrops, were the only family in Boston with
legitimate rights to display their heraldic crest. They were also one
of the few families that could joke about the Forbeses as parvenus.

My mother was warm, but not emotionally accessible, and I think my parents had a comfortable and convenient marriage with so many childhood friends and family friends in common as well as common family. My mother's sister Sukey married my father's first cousin Mark; thus we are both first (Saltonstall) and second (Forbes) cousins with their children. This cross-pollination is not unusual in our family and further reinforced similar family traditions and parenting styles. Both Mum and Dad were products, as well as avatars, of the benign-neglect school of parenting. I often felt that we four children were an inconvenience to them. Both were very decent people but neither was naturally suited to interacting with young children. Dad chose to spend his weekend time with us supervising our work clearing brush, splitting wood, mending walls, and mowing fields on our property. Mum was by no means domestic, and she streamlined her housekeeping duties so she, too, could spend more time outside. This meant that we lived on the same four meals served over and over, and all of our clothing went from dryer to an inherited eighteenth-century highboy dresser in the laundry room, where we all would gather in the morning to pull miscellaneous underwear, socks, T-shirts, and pants out of the jumble. There was no clear title to most of this stuff, so it was best to show up early if you had your mind set on the blue underwear or the Beatles T-shirt. A housekeeper was on hand for the nastier chores, but we were expected to pitch in. This included fixing our own toilets and leaking radiators, as well as repairing loose tiles in bathrooms. Duct tape was the all-purpose remedy. All of this was framed in such lofty terms as self-reliance and character building, but the more direct message was "You are on your own." I was raised with a great sense of duty and responsibility, but there was no tenderness that pulled us together as a family. Working side by side was the way in which we showed intimacy.

Whenever we could break away from Dad's character-building chores, Mum would take us on "expeditions." Her favorite Saturday destination was the Milton town dump. I pulled a lovely red bicycle off the heap one year that was missing only one bumper. Laura, my youngest sister, spent her infancy in a crib that was the grand prize from one of these visits to the dump. If we behaved well on these trips, we would stop at Bent's Cookie Factory on the way home, where my mother would purchase a deeply discounted bag of broken cookies for us to eat as a treat. My parents would good-naturedly tease each other about which of their families had more members who were "a bit queer."

Whenever my mother pointed out how crazy the Forbeses were, my father would counter that the Saltonstalls simply covered their tracks by exiling their oddballs to faraway places and countries so nobody could see them. The Forbeses put theirs out to pasture at Naushon. When things grew really dire on either side, there was always McLean Hospital, where relatives would go for a "rest."

Objectively, the best that could be said about my father was that he was a nice man, that he was kind, intelligent, and cultured, a gentleman even when drunk. He was sensitive, which is not to say warm and nurturing, and he made great efforts to hide his vulnerabilities under a stoic veneer.

And yet, as my father, he was my hero, and adoring him was part of what my childhood idyll on Naushon was all about. In summer I would sit on the bow of our small outboard as we put-putted around the island and he taught me all the rocks in the channels and how to read the ripples in the water. When I was a little older, my uncle, who was a geology professor at UMass and spent every summer doing research in Labrador, bought a red freighter canoe named *Tanager*. With a twenty-horsepower Johnson, this became our WASP-eccentric motorboat. It must have been quite a sight to see all nine of us first cousins ages one through thirteen piled into this nineteen-foot canoe, each decked out in matching white tennis hats and scarlet T-shirts emblazoned with the boat's name in white iron-on letters. But antique charm meant nothing to me. I wanted an Aquasport with twin Evinrudes.

Our winter home, located on Harland Street in Milton, was a ten-bedroom mansion on a ten-acre estate with a clay tennis court and a big barn. There was no pool, but then we had a pond in the woods. It had been part of a much larger family property that Emerson's daughter Edith had subdivided. During the time that we lived there, we still shared a good deal of common land between the other houses that had remained in the family, which made for a greater feel of community and space. My great-great-uncle Alex built the house, which later passed to us in a swap with our aunt Charlotte, Alex's widow, who no longer needed such a huge place. Most of the furnishings were conveyed to us with the real estate. Our clan tended to furnish a house only once and even then mostly with repurposed family pieces in varying stages of decrepitude. To complete the decorating of the house, Mum and Dad purchased a grand total of two modern swivel chairs and a love seat for the library. Florence, Aunt Charlotte's daughter, had built another house on the property, and throughout my childhood, and much to my parents' chagrin, she would simply traipse through the old place—our place—as if it were still hers.

But Florrie was great fun for us kids. On snowy days she would hitch a wooden toboggan to one of her horses, which would pull

*My branch of the Forbes clan: Edith Emerson Forbes with her
children, their spouses, and her grandchildren.*

us at top speed around the snowy fields as we did our best to stay
on board. During the Christmas season, she and her husband,
Andy, would dress as Santa and Mrs. Claus and ride their horses
around the woods.

We had a family archive room in one of the upstairs bedrooms
originally designed for servants, and Florrie took considerable
care of filing family photographs, tintypes, glass plates, maps, and
papers there until they ultimately outgrew the space and were
taken to the Massachusetts Historical Society.

As a child, I took refuge in that dusty room to pore over the
family history. I wanted to know all about these long-since-
deceased relatives. Given that none of my living relatives really
spoke much about emotions, I tried to read their eyes and their
faces, as well as their written words, to see if I could learn anything more about them as people.

Another adjunct to our nuclear family was a man named Gerard who lived up on the second-floor servants' quarters. When I asked my father once who Gerard was and what he did, my father answered, "He came with the house." Curiously, my mother gave precisely the same response when, unsatisfied with my father's response, I asked her the same question. The best I could figure was that he kept the wood box filled, and one year he painted the cellar. The only other thing I knew about him was that he came from Nova Scotia.

My mother believed in what she called the "two door" theory—two doors between the parents and the kids—so, when we were small, my brother Jamie, my sister Heidi, and I were up in tiny garret rooms with rusty iron bed frames and horsehair mattresses just down the hall from Gerard. To make my room cheery, my mother agreed to paint the entire room—walls and ceiling—bubblegum pink. She then acquiesced to painting a roll-top desk inherited from her grandmother Ayer the same color pink. She even added my initials in purple. Because of my mother's indulging my outlier desire for color, fresh paint, and design, this was the one moment in my childhood when I felt special and loved.

But this tiny room was also the place that brought home to me just how much "You're on your own" meant that I was going to have to provide my own nurturing. One scorching hot and still summer afternoon I was trying to unlock the sole window to let in some air when the sash cord snapped and the top section of windows slammed down like a guillotine. Or more luckily, like a bear trap, because all ten of my eight-year-old fingers were caught beneath it with no hope of escape. I felt like a witch in the stocks at Salem. The house was large enough that hollering for help would have been futile, and, truth be told, I feared raising my voice for fear of violating the Way of the WASP. I knew it would be a good long time before I was missed and someone came to look for me, but I stayed there mutely resigned to my fate. I recall only that my legs were very tired from standing by the time my brother Jamie finally came to tell me it was time for supper.

Gerard had a television—we did not—so Jamie and I would sneak in to watch the Bruins and *Lost in Space*. Downstairs we had an old-fashioned kitchen, with butler's pantry, larder, full-wall iron coal stove, and service area. Gerard would sit alone in the larder and have his meals. I would hear the sound of his cutlery on his plate as he ate silently in the pantry night after night and I would wonder if he was lonely. He never seemed to be. He, too, seemed bereft of emotion, though I do recall he had a quiet sense of humor and would laugh without opening his mouth.

Gerard had a friend named Fred who also had a long history with our family and had been one of the caretakers back in Uncle Alex's day. Fred was retired and also lived on the property, sometimes tinkering with the tractors. Fred had been a lifetime employee of the Forbes family. As a young boy, he was a cabin boy on William Hathaway Forbes's 108-foot schooner *Merlin*, and in later years he was a stable groom for William's son Ralph. My father Ralph, grandson of the previously mentioned Ralph, remembers Fred driving him by sleigh on winter days to attend classes at Milton Academy. Fred would also lead the entire family horse herd, he on horseback, from Milton to New Bedford each year to catch the steamer over to Naushon for the summer and then retrace his steps in late October. We leased out the pastures for sheep, and a few of our neighbors boarded horses with us, so there was still a modicum of agricultural work to be done.

It never occurred to me at the time that any of these living arrangements were odd. Swapping houses. Living down the hall from a retired handyman who'd been passed along like a serf. A communal clothing in the laundry room in shared drawers. A family archive hidden in a dusty wing of the house until it was carted away to a museum.

But then when I was about ten I finally got my chance to be "normal." My father was appointed special assistant to William Simon, secretary of the treasury in the Ford administration, and we moved to the D.C. area for two years. We went to public school in Montgomery County, we lived in a tract house in Bethesda, and I loved it. I had friends with names like Vickie, Dabber, and Chrissie. Our neighbors were not only within walking distance, they were within shouting distance!

In her New England frugality, my mother decided to bring only essentials, and she had them packed in wooden crates for reuse for our return move. These wooden crates served as bases for our mattresses, side tables, and even the front entry table and coffee table in our living room.

In a town that had less of an appreciation of old Boston culture, her thrift was seen as poverty. I was teased regularly in the schoolyard that our family was so poor that we couldn't even afford furniture.

I coveted the coziness and sameness of the houses on our Bethesda street, all mirror images of each other on tiny lots. Instead of inhabiting a photo spread from *Town & Country*, all riding clothes and Labrador retrievers, I wanted to live American life the way it appeared in the sitcoms on TV. In Bethesda, we were there, with a two-car garage, a television that no longer was stored in the closet when not in use, and a freight train running practically through our backyard. To my greatest delight, we even had an ice-cream truck that drove down our street on hot summer nights.

But all this ordinariness, even faux poverty, was in marked contrast to the family picnics we enjoyed at cabinet softball games, or the quiet dinners we had with dignitaries and government officials. We thought it was great fun when Bill Simon and Francine Neff came to dinner one night and we compared their signatures on paper napkins to the ones they had made on the newly minted U.S. currency.

After only a couple of years, though, we came back from Washington and my father went back to the bank and to the rest of his old Boston accoutrements, which included a great deal of gin and cigarettes. All through childhood I remember him arriving home after we'd eaten, then sitting down with a martini, and then the sound of the ice clinking in the glass as he came up the stairs many martinis later. He'd get slurry late at night, but never out of control. But after Washington he began to decline, and the once comforting sound of the ice clinking and the stairs creaking took on an ominous cast. I'd worry when I'd hear the car come in that he wouldn't make it up the steps. Then I'd worry when I didn't hear the car come in at all.

In Forbes family fashion we simply carried on as if nothing were the matter. Each Sunday we would take our mile-long walk in the woods behind the house, traversing through the beautiful stand of trees that Great-Great-Uncle Alex had planted in a grid, then around the pond, and then over the stone bridge that spanned the brook where we'd play Pooh Sticks, dropping twigs over one side, then seeing how long it would take them to get to the other, à la Winnie the Pooh.

For me, these woods were the next best thing to Naushon. They provided a sanctuary where I could feel something other than the numbness and emptiness that haunted me. I was aware of my own detachment from my emotions, but detached I remained. Whenever I'd have a flash of sadness, I'd remind myself of the Forbes/Saltonstall lesson learned all too well: *You can't cry—that's weakness*. So instead I'd bottle it up.

My usual recourse was to sit in our stand of trees or to lie in the field nearby and feel close to God. It was all very Emersonian, without any reference to Emerson. Nobody told me, "God is here; this is our church." Nobody talked about such things. Religion was pro forma like everything else, with the family attending services on Christmas and Easter. Many of my friends were having bat mitzvahs and confirmations and other religious rites of passage. The rites of passage that passed down in my family with reverence seemed to be attending the fall and spring "sheeping" and being invited to the autumn hunt or passing your sailing test to be able to captain one of the Herreshoff twelve-footers at the boat dock. At around this time I changed my affiliation from Unitarian to Episcopalian. It was hardly a radical shift, but the Anglicans had prettier churches, and I wanted something less abstract.

I was also desperate for structure. When I was twelve, my father handed me the car keys. I had learned to drive a tractor as a child, and he said, "It's the same idea. You'll figure it out." I didn't want to figure out how to drive an old pea-green Volvo with floor mats strategically placed to hide the rust holes in the floor. We could see pavement through those holes and no amount of heat in winter could ever make that car warm enough. My father adored that car, but I longed for the wood-paneled station wagons driven by the families in the planned community down the street and back in Washington. I wanted to fit in. In my young life it seemed there had been far too much "figure it out." I wanted somebody in charge. I wanted more God, and definitely more adult supervision.

Unfortunately, this was the seventies, and the culture was moving from Emersonian self-reliance to simple self-indulgence. Neighborhood parties increasingly involved bonfires, lots of alcohol and cigarettes for the parents, as well as pot. At one Sunday evening neighborhood gathering I walked through the living room of a neighbor's home and found a large pile of marijuana in the center of the floor, covered by a tarp. Their father, my cousin, had harvested it from their garden earlier that afternoon.

And then there was the night on Naushon when I was coming up the path from the beach and heard singing coming from the outdoor shower at Shore House. There must have been ten people in there, my parents and their friends, all clearly overserved at cocktail hour and beyond.

My father had developed a roving eye, and my mother's primary mode of coping through tough times was neighborhood high jinks. She put a "Loch ness monster" in the pond, to be discovered at the bottom when we drained it. Pink flamingos would appear on our neighbor's front yard. I think this was striving to survive, even be creative and clever, within the confines of a numbing marriage that was now officially falling apart.

Mum attributes my father's breaking out of the traces to his time in Washington. His job in the Treasury Department had been the first time he'd really been tested, the first time his pedigree alone could not carry him through. It was not long before he left Bank of Boston and went to work at J. M. Forbes and Company, managing the family assets. This involved much smaller numbers but far more hand-holding, a task for which my father was not well adapted.

I remember one day sitting in the tiger lilies in the backyard when a Cabot cousin said, "Everybody knows your father is having an affair with Amy." I was twelve or so at the time and a student at Milton Academy, and this was news to me. Amy was a teacher at the school. She was also my mother's best friend.

It was not long afterward that my nine-year-old sister called me to say Mum and Dad were in therapy. How nice, I thought; they're working on their relationship. I don't know if that naïveté was real or an attempt to blunt the anxiety that was beginning to overwhelm me.

During this time my mother began a period of self-discovery. She went on Esalen retreats, started speaking New Age Goddess Movement psychobabble, and was more physically demonstrative with us, although the obvious awkwardness of it on both sides made it difficult for me to receive the loving overtures in the way they were intended. When she told me that she loved me one day, I was mortified. All day I wanted to crawl out of my skin. That evening at dinner I could not look her in the eye because the intimacy that she shared with me was so uncomfortable. This open, sharing creature was not my mother and bore no resemblance to my other relatives. Deeply lonely and looking for acceptance, I wanted to like the sudden attention, but it frightened me.

On the night of my thirteenth birthday my parents were out with Amy and I was feeling sorry for myself. It was my birthday, after all, and I was all alone. I was sorry that my parents had chosen not to be with me, and sorrier still that they had chosen to be with Amy. For just a moment, a stab of profound sadness went through me. I felt tremendously empty and disengaged, hopeless, and the fear of feeling more emotion overwhelmed me. Perhaps my adolescent brain formulated the thought that a person who felt like this would probably kill herself.

This thought sent a tremor of fear throughout my body. I was sitting on the floor outside the library at home, and I picked up the black rotary phone to call my parents at the restaurant. But then I started calling other people instead, beginning with my cousin Beth, but I couldn't reach anyone. I was desperate to connect with someone, but too scared to wake my brother, still fearful that any display of emotional excess would land me in McLean.

Eventually I got in bed, and I started having these images of going down to the kitchen and picking out a knife and plunging it into my chest. I even knew which knife—it had a rusted blade (my mother still has it in her kitchen; I use it regularly)—and the vividness of the image made me so terrified I might do it that for the longest time I remained wide awake, all the more terrified that if I dozed off I might sleepwalk and actually go downstairs and kill myself. I thought of writing a note saying, "I don't want to die. It was a mistake," and as I began to compose the note in my head, mercifully, I dropped off.

I think the most significant issue that deterred me from killing myself was my concern about the terrible mess it might make. I didn't want to be so much trouble, and I certainly didn't want to disappoint my parents with my loss of emotional control. It never occurred to me that they might be sad if I died. I was only concerned that killing myself would present an inconvenience to them and I wondered how they would explain my death to friends and family.

The next day I told my mother, but her reaction—she looked at me wide eyed, as if thinking, "Oh my god, my daughter's going insane"—gave me yet another cause for panic. This was, of course, my worst fear that she was validating. With my schizophrenic grandmother, and all the disdain for emotion, I was sure they would lock me up in no time.

I could see that my mother wanted to be there for me, but she simply didn't know how. I felt bad for her that she was so ill equipped. But at least she got me to go see the school counselor, who assured me that everything I was feeling was "normal" for girls my age. Her reassurance allowed me to open up into a crying jag or two, during which I told her that all I wanted was to not feel numb. Again, her counsel was that this was all very normal for girls my age. "Now, is there anything else I can help you with?"

Shortly thereafter my father staged an uncharacteristically extravagant fortieth birthday bash for my mother, with limos and a boat, and shortly thereafter the affair with Amy became broadly known. Consequently, my mother stayed in Milton and my father took an apartment on Commercial Wharf in Boston. Following the divorce, they sold the house, and I never felt that I had a secure place with either of my parents. It's really no wonder that Naushon feels like home.

That first summer back from California, our long residence on Naushon in July had given us a chance to get back in touch with the rhythms of the place, which include not just the seasons and the tides, but all manner of living things. For two hundred years, the first event each day has been letting the sheep out of their night pens, then gathering around for breakfast on the lawn. This is followed by the parade in front of the house at seven, when our herd of thirty-two horses is let out to pasture. They all walk and trot in a line through a large red gate, across the meadow and into the stable

Horses in pasture, Naushon Island.

to get their breakfast. Being Forbes horses, they have a strong sense of tradition—a herd order that they always follow—with Jax in the lead and Blitzen bringing up the rear.

In 1995, two years after Michael and I were married, we assumed responsibility for Mansion House, a pleasure—and a financial burden—we shared with my sister Heidi and her husband Bjorn. One of thirty or so family homes now on the island, the place was huge, and pretty ramshackle, and we could have bought quite a nice new house for the cost of the deferred maintenance projects we launched into. At first, when the rain came through the roof, we simply set out washbasins and leather "fire brigade" buckets. One of these had become the resting place for a mummified seabird. I checked the date stamped into the leather. It was 1797.

Built in 1809, the full house didn't have electricity throughout until the 1950s, and some of the wiring put in at that time still remains. The kitchen and backstairs rooms were hooked up first in the mid-1920s, and then only because of complaints from the servants. To the old-line gentry of my grandparents' generation, electric lights in a summer place seemed somehow wrong, a frill unbecoming to a true Yankee.

In the mid-1800s, to the basic Federal architecture John Murray Forbes had added an east wing, including a billiard room. A west wing came along in the late 1800s, and then my great-great-uncle Cam, John Murray Forbes's grandson, added staff rooms, a four-story elevator to a widow's walk, and an observatory. By the time his nephew (my grandfather David) took over, much of this had fallen into disrepair, so David simply hacked off about a third of the place. But that still left a lot of old house weathering winter storms and summer salt air. We re-clapboarded the front, added a new porch, updated several bathrooms, and put on a new roof.

In purely economic terms this made no sense, but Mansion House has always been a labor of love. It's built on a hill surrounded by sheep meadows and horse pastures, and yet it sits right in the center of things, with its veranda providing a commanding view of the tiny harbor. Anyone traveling up island must pass along one of the trails in front or back, so sitting out on the porches on summer mornings, I have come to learn the walk of almost every family member and frequent visitor.

The island has eighteen full-time employees to maintain the animals and the houses, and a fair amount of infrastructure held in common. There's a small power plant and an ancient, privately owned telephone system—after all, we bankrolled Alexander Graham Bell—which nobody uses, neighbors preferring to simply drop by for a chat. In case of fire there's also an old pump

Mansion House in 1917, after the addition of the east and west wings.

truck, but if it came right down to it, the Forbes procedure for
dealing with conflagration could be summed up as hot dogs and
marshmallows.

Family tradition on the island included ways of doing without
or supplementing that were either incredibly creative or deliber-
ately perverse, depending on your point of view. We cooked up
new rules to deal with ancient card decks, board games, and puz-
zles that were missing pieces. In grade school I took a page from
Scarlett O'Hara and pulled down a panel of curtains to make a
dress for a dance.

My mother, not predisposed in any way to vanity, was not a
fan of the party dress. At age ten I was put on a monthly allow-
ance of twenty-five dollars, which was to cover all of my clothing
and personal expenses. Compared with what my peers received,
that number was low even before factoring in the cost of clothing.
For a girl like me who was rapidly developing an eye for designer
blue jeans and had discovered that clothes could come from places

other than the four-inch-thick Sears Roebuck catalog and L.L. Bean, this was a challenge. So I learned to sew.

To this day the ladies' smoking room is missing one window's worth of fabric, while the remaining nine sections have been identified as "important" in Early American textiles and may be bound for a museum.

On the Sunday of Members Meeting weekend 2004, we had a concert in the green room of Mansion House with two of my cousins on violin and cello. While they were playing, a squall blew in, and Charlotte loved storms. After the music was over I found her standing on the porch, eyes raised to the thunderous heavens, arms and chest out, letting sheets of water run off the roof and onto her face. She was in ecstasy.

Another Forbes tradition was that everyone should write in the guest book at the end of each visit. The leather-bound volumes date back to 1842. I wrote a long entry at the end of our stay in July, and I knew we'd be back soon. This was our life now. We'd be back all the time, making new memories to mingle with the old as the years unfolded blissfully into the future.

4

Summer Ends

Our trip home from Naushon that night was the perfect end-of-summer-weekend experience. There was a special freshness in the air after the storm, and it was time to think about a new school year, and new beginnings for all of us.

Just off the ferry at Woods Hole we had a seafood dinner at the adjacent restaurant, then piled into the car, the three kids heading into that beautiful twilight sleepy zone for the drive back up to Weston. As Michael drove, I sang the kids to sleep. "The Circle Game." "Both Sides Now." I specialized in the sixties folk songs from Joni Mitchell and Carole King and Judy Collins. I remember thinking very consciously at the time what a perfect family moment this was. Vigilant Dad at the wheel, Mom singing soothing songs by his side, the kids safe and warm and piled up like kittens in the backseat, able to wake up the next morning as if by some miracle in their own beds at home. This seemed like the most precious gift. I remember hoping that the children would imprint these sensations as well, remembering this as the apotheosis of a beautiful, carefree childhood.

The next morning, a Monday, August 16, the kids found a mouse and I helped them build a little house for it in a shoe box. Charlotte was excited about the new pet, but otherwise was a little listless. I felt her forehead and her temperature seemed normal, so I encouraged her to go on to camp, which she did.

Everyone passed through their day as usual, but that afternoon, when the kids went back to the shoe box to check on the mouse, it was dead. A dead "pet" meant that we had to have a funeral and interment, but no one seemed unduly concerned. We sang "Kumbaya" and buried the shoe box. No tears. The next day, though, around midmorning, one of the camp counselors called me at home. "Mrs. Bigham . . ."

Charlotte had dug up the dead mouse, put it in her pocket, and brought it with her to camp. I never got the chance to ask her why she did this. It did cross my mind, though, her great-great-great-great-grandfather's reopening that crypt, his statement that he "just had to see."

Later, when I picked her up that afternoon, she was preoccupied with a boy in a wheelchair waiting nearby. I tried to make her stop staring at him, but she was obviously very upset about his disability. On the way home we talked about it, and she said it made her sad to think of any small child not being able to run and play.

At bedtime that evening Charlotte wanted her sippy cup and an extra snuggle. She wanted me to cradle her in my arms as if she were a baby. She wanted extra Mommy time, all of which I gave her, but not without a bit of exasperation. I had two other children to take care of as well, and Charlotte was always the one who wanted a different kind of dinner, an extra bottle, an extra story, or an extra snuggle. She was also the one who would beg me to sign her up for a ballet class and then, after I'd driven for an hour to get her there, wouldn't get off my lap.

I made it a habit to check the kids in the middle of the night, and it felt like she might have had a slight fever, but she was sleeping soundly, so I let it go. I had become a master of the Motrin and Tylenol mix Annie had recommended to us in North Carolina two years before, but I didn't want to wake her for medication unless it was absolutely necessary.

On Wednesday morning when we woke up it was clear that Charlotte was really not feeling well. She was draggy and droopy and warm to the touch, so I began to administer the over-the-counter medicines. She had a good appetite—she ate four pieces of cinnamon toast for breakfast—so I wasn't overly concerned. My dominant concern about Charlotte's health at that moment was still the issue of irregular muscular development, the overdeveloped legs, and the clumsiness that we'd seen developing in California.

She asked me to put her hair up in pigtails, and my own as well, which of course I did. She said it made us look like twins, so we pretended to be twins, big and little. Then she put on Michael's shirt—a blue jean jacket with flannel lining—and sat down to watch TV. She wanted me to watch with her, but I loathe television, so I tried to make her comfortable and let her watch on her own. She'd be staying home today, all day, so we'd have plenty of time to be together.

Michael had an early morning golf game, so he dropped Cabot and Beatrice off at camp on the way to the course. Charlotte rested and I puttered about, and three hours later Michael called from his office and asked us to come by and bring him a jacket. He was in a new, makeshift space in an office park and he hadn't figured out yet how to regulate the air-conditioning. This was in nearby Newton, just off the Massachusetts Turnpike and Route 128, the ring road around Boston that bills itself as "America's Technology Highway."

Charlotte seemed to be doing okay with just her little touch of fever, so we headed out to the car with her still wearing the huge blue jean jacket and a pair of my flip-flops. It wasn't until we climbed into the station wagon that I remembered about the squirrel. We'd had the car shipped from California when we moved in June, and the driver traveled with a pet squirrel—an idea that Charlotte loved. But the animal had enjoyed a pretty free run, and after the car arrived we'd found little squirrel pellets in and all around the upholstery. In short, the interior smelled like squirrel shit.

We drove over with the windows open, the car stinking to high heaven, and when we got to Michael's office I gave Charlotte a piggyback ride in. We delivered the jacket, took a look around, and then it was time to head home.

As we got back to the car I put my hand on Charlotte's forehead and she still felt warm. We'd had plenty of fevers since the big scare in North Carolina, but her temp had always responded to the home remedies. This time, however, it wasn't coming down. It didn't feel alarmingly high—it just wasn't coming down.

A friend had recommended a medical practice in town, Pediatric Associates, and even before we moved we'd had the kids' records transferred. We'd been assigned a doctor, but as yet we'd never visited. This seemed like the time.

As we pulled out of Michael's parking lot I dialed the number on my cell phone, and when the assistant answered I described the situation and told her that we'd like to come in.

"Okay," she said. "Let's see . . . there's an opening at three."

"No. Actually . . . I'd like to come by right now."

I was surprised by my own adamancy. In the larger health care scheme of things, having to wait a few hours for an appointment for a child with a fever was perfectly acceptable—no big deal. But something was pushing me.

"I'm afraid three is the best we can do," she said.

"Uh, look . . . ," I said, but then I took a deep breath. Every time I tried to explain our concerns about nontriggered malignant hyperthermia people looked at me like I was crazy. "My sister-in-law is the head of pediatric anesthesiology at the University of Maryland," I started in. "We had an incident a couple of years back and . . . well, my sister-in-law thinks—"

At which point the call dropped. I was at a stoplight, and once again my gut took over. I was in no mood to fight this particular battle over a bad mobile connection, so rather than push redial, I simply put down the phone, turned right instead of left, and headed immediately toward Newton-Wellesley Hospital. The day care/summer camp where Beatrice was enrolled was on the way, and her day ended at noon, so I stopped to pick her up, and then we continued on to the emergency room.

The child I presented at the admitting desk had a temperature of 102, which was hardly the stuff of medical drama. The staff looked a little askance, and they listened politely as I asked them to do a neurology workup. They nodded as I expressed my concern about the odd muscular changes Charlotte had been experiencing, as well as the clumsiness. Then I observed them observing me, and I could see that they weren't quite sure what to do.

I was cool as a cucumber, but every bit as insistent as any screaming hysteric. And yet what I was saying didn't make any sense. I think that deep down in my unconscious I was scared to death that Charlotte's fever wasn't coming down, but in my own mixture of denial, confusion, and frustration I wasn't willing to go into the whole malignant hyperthermia saga. I didn't want to be dismissed as that neurotic Internet Mom with too much time on her hands. I'd save malignant hyperthermia for the resident. But what I'd chosen to express concern about—Charlotte's neuromuscular development—was not an issue for the ER.

For several minutes I went back and forth with the woman at the desk, not getting very far, and then Charlotte simply wilted, slid down my leg, and lay on the floor.

"Charlotte, get up!" I said. I was having an Embarrassed Mommy moment to match my Crazy Mommy anxieties. Then she vomited.

A nurse hurried from behind the desk. She helped me comfort my daughter and begin to clean her up. Then she led us back to a curtained room, where we got Charlotte out of her messy clothes and onto the examining table. The nurse took Charlotte's temperature, pulse, and so on, gave her some Valium, then said that the doctor would be in to see us in a moment. Beatrice and I were then left to help Charlotte pick out a princess video to watch while we waited.

Whether it was the drug or simply being taken care of in a comfortable bed, Charlotte seemed to relax. Beatrice, barely three, was more or less oblivious.

With Charlotte resting and Beatrice on my lap, I then made the first round of phone calls to Michael, to my mother, and to my brother. I left the same message for each of them. "Charlotte's not well. We're at Newton-Wellesley. Just wanted you to know."

At which point I think I relaxed, too. I could feel my shoulders loosening up a bit and my blood pressure coming down. This was a Harvard teaching hospital—the best medical care in the country. We'd be here a few hours and before we left we'd be on our way to getting some solid answers.

About ten minutes later a doctor came in, introduced himself, and asked what seemed to be the trouble. Here was my chance to fully explain what was on my mind.

He looked at the chart, then said, "I see vomiting . . . a bit of a fever . . ." Then he looked at Charlotte. "How're you feeling?" he asked.

"Fine," she whispered. Then he looked into her eyes, listened to her lungs, palpated her abdomen.

As he gave Charlotte the once-over, I told him about North Carolina and the rush to the emergency room. I told him about Anne—her immediate intervention, and her suspicions about malignant hyperthermia.

"That's usually a surgical complication," he said.

"I know. We think she has the nontriggered kind."

He washed his hands and sat down and made a few notes on his clipboard. Then he asked me to take him through the North Carolina experience again. He nodded as I repeated the story, and he made more notes. I couldn't tell if I was really getting through, but at least he wasn't rolling his eyes.

Finally he said, "Why don't you give me a number where I can reach your sister-in-law. I'll also check with the pediatric anesthesia people here."

I gave him the number from my book; then he smiled and stepped out.

This was good. At last we were going to put all the pieces of the puzzle on the same table and figure out what was wrong with my daughter.

I phoned Michael and again left a message. "We're still here," I said. "Call me when you can."

Then I glanced over at Charlotte. She looked flushed and very uncomfortable. I also noticed that her masseter muscle had begun to twitch, the same jaw muscle that had signaled the crisis in North Carolina.

I pushed the call button and a nurse came back in. She took one look at Charlotte's red cheeks and gave her a quick temperature reading. Her fever had spiked.

Then all hell broke loose. She pushed a button and I heard "Code Blue" over the intercom.

A second nurse came in and suggested that Beatrice go with her to get some ice cream down the hall. My throat tightened as Charlotte's eyes locked onto mine and I saw the fear. She seemed to be telling me that she'd been in this place before and she knew what was about to happen. Then her eyes took on that vacant stare I'd seen at the beach house on the Outer Banks. Her feet began to curl just the way they'd done two years before. Her jaw clenched even more and her head began to turn to the side.

Doctors came running. Nurses came in and packed her in ice, irrigating her colon with cold water. My heart was pounding, yet I remained outwardly calm, dry eyed. I seemed to have stepped outside my body, leaving only the rational part there in the room, functioning at a minimal level. I was engaged and responsive, dealing with the situation, but I couldn't feel anything.

They decided to move Charlotte to a room just down the hall, one with more equipment.

Chiefs of services began crowding in: Pediatrics. Neurology. Anesthesiology. I kept glancing at the clock. Her fever had been at 107 or 108 for eleven minutes now. I asked the head of pediatrics how long this could go on before permanent damage. Her vague and evasive response confirmed my worst fears.

With fingers trembling I made a second round of calls and reached my brother. "It's not looking good," I said. "I need you to call Mum."

I reached Michael's mother, Betty, told her what was happening. I asked her to call Anne and Harry to get the updates and to stay in touch. I tried Michael again but his cell must have been switched off. I asked the nurse to help me and somehow the hospital got in touch with the police, who went to look for my husband.

There were so many people hovering around Charlotte's bed now that, even though I was holding her hand, she couldn't see me. I stayed very close to her ear and kept talking and singing to her as the doctors worked. I was trying to comfort her and assure her that I was by her side. They had an IV line inserted into her arm, and a resident came in to administer dantrolene, the antidote Annie had told us about. This was reassuring, but also terrifying. This was North Carolina all over again. And as Annie had warned us, dantrolene didn't always work. There was no magic bullet.

I heard Charlotte shriek, "I want my mummy!" It was the last thing she ever said.

They put a plastic mask over her face with a bag beneath it and a doctor squeezed the bag to force air into her lungs. Then they made a small opening in her throat and inserted a tube with oxygen. Then I realized they were doing CPR. For the next forty-five minutes the doctors took turns pushing on her chest. I continued to hold her hand, singing the song about walking in the rain by your side. I found myself muttering each time I finished a verse, "Please don't go. I love you so much, please don't go." Then I would start to sing again, my lips almost touching her ear.

I thought about the rain on Naushon three days earlier and how much she'd loved that storm. I thought about the dead mouse she'd taken to camp and her concern for the boy in the wheelchair. I thought about all the things Charlotte was and I thought this can't be happening. She can't be dying because she has so much living she has to do. With us. With her family. In this world. We have so many things we need to tell her, so many experiences we have yet to share with her. We're not done yet. Not by a long shot. This was my "difficult child," feisty and headstrong. We were just beginning to understand each other.

They monitored her blood continuously, and the level of oxygen reaching her brain wasn't good. I continued to sing, and I continued to hold her hand, but I became increasingly aware of the nagging internal voice telling me that—best case—the little girl who'd asked for extra hugs last night was never coming back the same as before.

Conscious. Unconscious. Rational. Emotional. There was no longer any part of me that could hide from what was happening. I stopped saying, "Please don't go." My mantra became simply, "I love you. I'm here. I love you. I love you." She shouldn't have to linger just to comfort her parents, not if she didn't want to. I wanted her to know how much she was loved. The rest was up to her.

The police had found Michael. He rushed in looking dazed and terrified, and I was immensely relieved, for his sake mostly. He stood over her bed and did what I could not bring myself to do, which was to stare directly into her face, bloated from the fluids and the CPR. He leaned down and kissed her and whispered a few words of comfort, but then he was so overcome that he had to step back out into the hall. The doctors and the nurses briefed him. There was nothing but bad news.

He spoke with Anne, who was on the line from Maryland, and when he came back into the room he asked for a priest to say last rites. The best they could manage was a protestant chaplain. She arrived and began to say prayers at the foot of the bed. I couldn't listen. I wanted her to go away. My body was already numb, and now my mind started going numb as well, overwhelmed by a kind of white noise. More and more I was floating up above the reality inside this hospital room. My child wasn't dying. Why was this stranger mumbling at the foot of the bed? She wasn't even a Catholic. She was annoying to me; was she at all helping Michael? He seemed oblivious to her presence.

When I came back down from my out-of-body moment, the doctors were still taking turns pounding on Charlotte's chest. I saw Michael standing in the doorway. My husband who was always so in command looked small and fragile and utterly broken. He looked at me and held my gaze as he said haltingly but resolutely "Call it off. Stop it." He was talking to the doctors.

They stopped the CPR and stepped back from the bed. A nurse turned off the monitors. Another removed the IV and clipped the oxygen tube. Then all the medical personnel began to drift out of the room until it was just the three of us—Michael and me and our dead child suspended in a killing silence.

I was so cold I was shaking all over, but otherwise I sat utterly rigid, listening as the hum of the fluorescent lights became unbearably loud. Michael crumbled and started to weep. He threw himself completely into his grief with no inhibitions. He climbed into the bed beside our little girl and began to sob uncontrollably.

I had no idea what to do, so I stayed exactly where I was, sitting rigid next to Charlotte, holding her hand. I watched, detached but envious of my husband. He had such immediate access to his tears as he lay there and cried and held her and stroked her hair.

I became fixated on the warmth leaving her body. How could I keep her warm? Should I lie on top of her, too? Wrap her in more sheets?

After a while it became clear to me that the body lying there was only that: a body. Charlotte—her soul, her essence—had moved on. Just as I was unsure of the exact moment that life left her I was also not sure of the moment her soul slipped out of her body. They did not seem to leave at the same time. It was only as that realization began to settle in—that both had left her body—that I could let go of her hand.

A nurse came back in and Michael got to his feet and pulled himself together, but he didn't return to his usual posture. The strong and confident Michael of yesterday was gone. He looked diminished, shattered and defeated. He looked the way I thought I ought to feel. The only feeling I could access was a physical sense of having been eviscerated. I felt as though my innards had been removed and I was an empty vessel, devoid of any feeling or emotion that could connect me to humanity. In those first few moments I was an automaton moving in circles and waiting for the next directive.

"I'll go see about Beatrice," Michael said. Then he added, "I'll call the family."

I sat waiting for the bolt of lightning. It never came. There was no drama. My world had simply stopped.

The nurse turned to me and asked if we wanted footprints. I said yes.

Handprints? Yes.

She went to get the paper.

I still had no idea what to do, or how to act, but when the nurse came back I told her I wanted a cast of Charlotte's foot. I don't know why the thought popped into my head, but she had such beautiful feet. The nurse said it wasn't such a good idea.

"I want her pigtails," I said. The nurse handed me a pair of scissors.

Slowly, painstakingly, I cut off the little sprigs of blond hair and put them in my bag. Then I lifted up one of the pigtails Charlotte had put my own hair in that morning, and brought the scissors up to cut that off as well. The nurse reached up and took the scissors out of my hand. Neither of us said a word.

I closed my eyes and stroked Charlotte's face, tracing the outline of her nose, her ears, running my fingers over her brow line like a mother inspecting her newborn, or a sculptor trying to get the details exactly right. I was trying to imprint her features in my memory. I was very aware that this would be the last time I would ever touch her.

It was at this moment of total stillness, of no sound but the buzzing of the lights, when Maria, our Peruvian nanny, came in, understandably very upset, and threw herself onto the bed next to my daughter's body. I was aware that her grief and shock, so emotionally expressed, had the effect of relegating me and my unwanted stoicism even further to the margins. In the welter of complicated feelings, I had the unwelcome one that she was acting like the proper mother and I was acting like a mere bystander. The Forbes steeliness came to the fore, though, and instead of screaming at her I calmly asked her to go help Michael with Beatrice, to go with him to pick up Cabot at summer camp, and to drive them all home.

She did leave, reluctantly, and for the first time the silence was complete.

So what do I do now? I was waiting for a sign, but none came. I knew that, eventually, the orderlies would come and take Charlotte down to the morgue. I'd already made the distinction between saying good-bye to my daughter and saying good-bye to her physical body. But then a wave of horror overtook me—the image of this person I loved being placed in a refrigerator with an identifying toe tag dangling off of her delicate six-year-old big toe.

Her clothes lay jumbled in the corner, and I reached over and picked up her sweater. I wanted her to be warm. But another part of me kept thinking, "Charlotte's not here anymore." It was only as I felt her body become cool and rigid that it became possible for me to leave. But not yet. This was my last chance. I climbed up onto the bed the way Michael had, but I still couldn't look at her. I didn't want her distorted face to be the last image I would have of her. I lay beside her and began to sob like Michael, but I felt like a bulimic putting a finger down my throat to purge. For the past three hours I had been in crisis mode, locked in my head, trying to be the responsible parent, on hand to watch over and comfort her and do whatever needed to be done. Now I was howling like a wounded animal, but it didn't feel like me. My WASP psyche was so at war with itself, not wanting to make a spectacle, not wanting to disturb anyone else in the hospital, yet desperate to fully feel and fully express the pain. Even the sobs from the now absent Maria seemed to indict me. Eventually I lay there in silence, pulling her to my belly with my arms around her, aware of the beating of my own heart and wishing that either mine, too, would stop or hers would start. Pleading to no one in particular that we could go back to the innocent and perfect state of hearts beating in unison when she had been floating in the protection of my womb.

I was still there beside Charlotte's body forty-five minutes later when Michael came back from bringing the kids home from camp. We didn't have much to say to each other, but after a while we joined hands—the three of us—and Michael and I said the Lord's Prayer. I spoke the words as earnestly as I could, but, again, it didn't feel like me. I did it for Michael.

Later, as we left the hospital, I went by the nurses' station to thank everyone individually. It became a receiving line, seven or eight people in a row. Some of the staff could not make eye contact. Most of them were crying, but not me. I felt very conscious of that. These people looked at me with great sympathy, and yet I was saying to myself, "I am a freak. They are crying. Why am I not the one crying?" The internal monologue had begun. "I'm not doing this right. How do you do this right?"

My brother Jamie, Charlotte's godfather, was waiting at the house when we arrived, along with Maggie Taylor from next door. She came over and gave me a hug. I knew that Maria was giving Beatrice and Cabot their dinner, and I also knew we had to tell them soon.

"I can't go in there," I said.

Maggie said, "Let's take a walk."

Jamie said he'd go back and stay with the kids while Maggie and Michael and I set off along the winding road that resembled a country road in Vermont, trying to collect our thoughts, trying to figure out what we were going to say to the kids. We said very little to each other, and the fact that my feet were stumbling forward was the only assurance I had that I was still conscious, still alive. Then I noticed the sun going down over my neighbor's big maple tree, and I felt an urgent impulse to tug it back up, or, like Superman trying to save Lois Lane, to make the earth spin backward. I didn't want this day to end, because this was the last day that Charlotte and I would ever be together. Charlotte was alive on August 18, 2004. Charlotte died on August 18, 2004. The fading of light into darkness has always seemed solemn and melancholy to me compared to the brightening promise of a sunrise. Never has the darkness lurking beyond that sunset seemed more frightening and empty. How could I turn the page on this day and how could I live in a tomorrow that would not have her in it?

When we came back up the driveway, Charlotte's godmother, Kim, one of my oldest school friends from Dana Hall, stood waiting for us. She lived in California now, and I wondered how she'd gotten here so fast. She'd been in New Hampshire with her family, she told me, and my sister had reached her by phone. She'd left her six-week-old infant with her mother up in Rye Beach to be with me.

Kim and I walked arm in arm into the mudroom, and I remember looking up on a shelf and seeing a pink cowgirl hat we'd bought for Charlotte on a trip to Nevada. The bizarre thought that crossed my mind was, "We have another daughter. Thank god we don't have to get rid of all our girl stuff."

I went upstairs and closed the door and called my friend Sarah back in California. She was a dear friend who just happened to be a therapist, but my urgency in reaching out to her was based more on the experience that we now shared. Three years earlier, her son Wyatt had died of a brain tumor.

"It's Sukey. Do you have time to talk?"

"Are you okay?" she asked me.

"Charlotte just died. You're the first person I've called."

"Oh, god . . . Oh, sweetie . . ."

I gave her a second to absorb the information. But I needed advice.

"How do I tell the kids? I don't know what to say to them."

"I'm so sorry. I'm just so sorry."

"How do I tell them? What's the best way?"

She was silent for a moment. Then she said, "Don't beat around the bush. Watch their reactions and try to respond. But there's no way to sugarcoat it."

We were both crying now. "I never should have had three kids," I blubbered. "I think I was overwhelmed. Maybe God's punishing me, you know? I just wasn't a good enough mother."

"Stop it. Don't beat yourself up. You're trying to take the blame. That's what children do when they're trying to make sense of something they can't possibly understand."

"I'm not a child."

"Just don't go there."

We talked for another moment, and she said she would fly east as soon as she could. I thanked her for her help, and then we hung up. Restless, I paced in a few small circles but in no particular direction. Then I went back downstairs.

We asked my brother to be with us when we told Cabot and Beatrice because we didn't know what was going to happen. Was I going to fall apart? Was Michael? I just felt we needed all hands on deck. We gathered everyone together and then we simply went in to the living room, sat down, and told them. My brother was silently crying the whole time, big tears streaming down his cheeks. Jamie had so much more access to his emotions than I did. It was almost as if he were experiencing the feelings for me. Empathy and feeling the pain of others has always come easily to me and I have no problem expressing emotion that is one step removed from me. Perhaps my brother and I share that. I imagined that if the tables had been turned and it had been me in Jamie's shoes that I might have the same access to the reservoir of sorrow. But this was too close.

Beatrice, only three, sat on Michael's lap, staring out as if we'd said we were having chicken for dessert. But Cabot was seven. His first response was, "You're lying. That didn't happen." He began to cry only when Michael started to cry.

"This can't be true," Cabot went on. "Why couldn't the doctors save her?"

"She had a special problem with fevers," I said. "You and Beatrice don't have that problem. You and Beatrice are going to be okay."

Then we all just sat there holding hands—Michael looking helpless, the kids looking bewildered, and I still feeling as if I were outside of my body, watching from the ceiling.

That night, when I put Cabot to bed, he said, "Give me a tickle massage." I rubbed his back and combed my fingers through his hair the way I had done each night since he was tiny.

I felt his little body relaxing, and then he asked me, "Who will I play all our Charlotte games with?"

"I'll play them with you," I said as I nuzzled his ear.

"No. You don't know them, and I can't teach you because they were our secret." My throat closed up and I was unable to speak.

Drawing him in to me, I spooned his back and lay with him, silently weeping for his loss of his adored sister until eventually he fell asleep. I was able to weep for his pain, but not for my own.

My own question was, "Where is she? Where has my daughter gone?"

My husband and all his relatives would tell me she was in heaven, but I just wasn't sure. All I knew was that I'd never be content until I had a better answer.

5

Reeling

That night, doped up on the Ambien for sleep and the Valium for anxiety that our doctor had prescribed, Michael and I struggled toward whatever rest we could find. Our house had an odd layout that required us to go through Charlotte's bedroom to reach our own and we weren't able to handle that, so we'd spread an air mattress on the floor of our upstairs sitting room. Before I finally nodded off, I wondered just how much Ambien it would take to sleep and sleep and sleep until I could one day wake up and be healed. Magical thinking had me wishing it could be that easy.

It seemed like only moments later that the midmorning sun woke me, sharp and bright, reflecting off the Tuscan yellow walls. A bird chirped merrily outside the window, and I remember thinking, "Shit. I'm alive."

During that first moment of awareness I thought about the weather, the mid-August in New England "makes you want to live forever" freshness and crispness, the perfect days of bright sun and no humidity and just a hint of autumn. This had always been my favorite time of year, and now I knew that I would always associate it with Charlotte's death.

I heard voices rising from the first floor, and my heart fell. It must be real, then. Yesterday had really happened, and now there would be people, and I just didn't have it in me to face them. But then again, I had to.

Michael and I put on the same clothes we had worn the

previous day and staggered downstairs, clinging to each other. I heard my cousin Beth's distinctive and comforting laugh. Beth always knew what to say or do and her laughter was a great vehicle for putting others at ease. She lived in Los Angeles, and I wondered how she had gotten to Boston so quickly. But then from the stairs I could see into the kitchen and it was filled with people— my mother and brother, Anne and Harry, Betty and Harry Senior—all with grief-stricken faces. Then I remembered the calls Michael said he was going to make after he'd left Charlotte's side. There had been night flights, early morning flights. This was definitely real.

Everyone stood as we entered the kitchen and there was a kind of group hug with murmurings of consolation, and all the while I was thinking how much I did not want this attention. I had already put on my game face, and now I was busily thinking about how I was going to be able to comfort these loved ones. Action was the only way I knew how to respond. They all seemed so shattered, and there was something about their sorrow that frightened me, because it confirmed just how awful this was. But I knew that part of their healing process was to be there for me, and so it was my obligation to perform for them, or so it seemed. My mother pulled me aside and said, "You're okay. Just do what you have to do."

Anne was cooking scrambled eggs for everyone, with Julie and Gracie helping serve. She asked me if I was hungry and I shook my head. From that moment on, about every half hour throughout the day someone would ask me if I wanted to eat something, and as often as not they would hand me a banana. Occasionally I would take a bite, then invariably spit it out. It was like trying to eat cotton.

I was greeting relatives, talking to children. But why was I not feeling the full weight of this? Why was I not falling apart? I was still an outsider in my own experience, drifting in and out of my body the way I had in the emergency room. The self-recrimination that I was "not doing this right" had settled in to stay, and the simple fact that I was alive seemed completely wrong.

I pulled Anne and Harry aside and said, "I can't handle this."

"No worries," Anne said. "We'll take care of everything."

And so they did. Organ donation, cremation—we gave Anne power of attorney. She asked to have Charlotte's body taken to Children's Hospital, where she felt the postmortem could be more sophisticated. She also wanted muscle tissue to go to a researcher in Bethesda. We agreed to both proposals.

Though staunch Catholics themselves, Anne and Harry were adamant that the Jewish tradition was on to something and that we needed to have the service as soon as possible. But this put even more pressure on logistics.

We moved out to the picnic table near the forge, where we could keep an eye on the kitchen, keep an eye on the children playing in the yard, and see people arriving. And people continued to arrive all day. Several more of my classmates from Dana Hall showed up early. Then Michael's sister, who had not set foot on an airplane since September 11, 2001, appeared with her two children. Michael's California brother was en route, along with his wife and kids. People were taking red-eyes from as far away as Australia. It seemed superhuman for our friends to make it from one side of the planet to the other so quickly, but then everything seemed surreal and out of joint that morning. I was incredibly touched by the outpouring, and yet I'd never felt more alone, or had more difficulty with just the basic business of staying alive. My chest felt as if there were steel bands holding it in like a coopered barrel. I had to work at filling my lungs, making the simple process of breathing conscious and deliberate. My extremities seemed very remote, and higher cortical functioning was just not happening.

I needed some help to absorb the loss. Leaving Charlotte at the hospital had seemed like the right thing to do at the time but now being at the house without her seemed so wrong. I was clear that what we'd left behind at the hospital was just a shell, as if her soul had grown too large for its container. Yet I wondered if we should have insisted on bringing her home. Bathing her. Anointing her with oils and sitting with her for a while. We had taken care of our little Sweetie Pea's every need for six and a half years plus the nine months she'd spent in the miracle of a baby's creation growing inside of me. Now we were supposed to hand her off to strangers to prepare her body for its next phase. I had a strong sense that we should have been the ones doing this work. Other cultures past and present do a better job with this, and in hindsight I now recognize how important it is for the bereaved to tend to the dead body. Death has become so sanitized in the Western world. We leave the preparations to the "experts." Bathing and tending to the body might have allowed the reality of the loss to wash over me. The tradition of anointing the body with oils made sense. Perhaps if I'd just gently caressed her body the way we always did during our bedtime snuggles or in quiet tender moments together, the experience would have seeped into my being and all of my senses. The rush of memories brought on by combing her hair, washing the arches of her dainty feet and the fingers of her small hands, dressing her, would have been a painful yet helpful transition. Instead she was yanked away. I let her go and I let someone else do that work. I saw no reason, at the time, to stay. But in hindsight I have a much deeper appreciation for what a gift it is to the bereaved to be more personally involved in preparing the body for burial or cremation or its final disposition. It gives the loss more of a chance to settle into the room. The souls still in this world need a bit more time to absorb the reality of death. I needed a more direct and physical experience with her body to allow myself to start to accept that she was gone. Instead, I was terribly, terribly stuck.

The best I could do was walk around like a zombie, signing for the endless floral arrangements being delivered to our door by one of the vans pulling up close to every ten minutes. It all seemed like a circus, or the Rose Bowl Parade. I felt guilty because I knew these flowers were all well intended, but I couldn't help hating them for what they represented: My child was dead. An even greater source of guilt was the fact that I was not behaving the way Michael was, with more visible expressions of grief. I felt my face locked in a flat and tight-lipped grimace that twitched now and then in an effort to show more emotion, but it just would not come. I desperately wanted to let my complete misery overtake me and yet I just as desperately feared that once it got hold of me I would lose all control. Michael and I were each getting up and down, moving from place to place, uncomfortable in our own skin, but in contrast to my stoic reserve he would sob and wail, then sit quietly with his shoulders slumped and his head hung low. I had never seen him in such visible pain. I had never seen anyone in such pain, and it moved me to want to protect him. But if I could feel his pain, why couldn't I feel my own?

For a while just after lunch I lost sight of him, and then a few minutes later he came to find me and said, "Come look at this."

I followed him back behind the forge. He pointed up into a big maple tree.

"That's my sign that Charlotte is okay," he said.

It was a fierce-looking red-tailed hawk, staring back at us as if she owned the place.

"It's been here all day," he said.

He stepped away to bring Cabot and Beatrice over to see the bird, and I just stood there staring at it. I'd always been a believer in signs, but I wasn't sure what the message was.

"Are you here for Charlotte?" I asked it out loud.

Michael came back with the kids and they joined me in watching the bird. My husband always had a very sensitive intuitive side, but he'd never lived his life that way. That's what made the next thing he said all the more surprising.

"We were chosen by God to be Charlotte's parents," he said.

I was too astounded to respond. I simply looked at him, listening intently.

"I think she came here to get what she needed," he added, "and then she had to move on."

He then turned his red-rimmed eyes toward me, staring at me with an expression every bit as fierce as the hawk's. "What she needed was a happy childhood."

What he was saying was completely illogical, and yet it all made perfect sense to me . . . everything except the fact that this mystical observation was coming from my extremely rational and analytical husband. And yet, coming from him, this assessment of what was "really" going on took on added weight, as if to confirm my own premonition. I actually entertained that this had not come from him but rather he had been the medium for a message

delivered from someone else. I had always put great faith in everything that Michael said. As incongruous as this was with his personality, this slightly cryptic, more than a little mystical pronouncement
made perfect sense and resonated immediately with me.

One of my friends from school was a tech guru, and she took
charge of hacking into our computers and sending out e-mails to
everyone we knew, notifying them of Charlotte's death. My cousins and my old friends represented more or less all the stages of
my life, and thus they were able to access just about everyone who
needed to know, which saved me many awkward phone calls and
painful explanations later.

This same team sat down at the kitchen table with Anne and
Harry and worked out prayer cards, programs, transportation,
and caterers, even selecting which photographs to display at the
service. Kim, Charlotte's godmother, had grown up in Weston,
so she found hotels for the out-of-towners, lined up babysitters,
and took the lead on finding a church. Anne and Harry made the
final choice, visiting each site, even "liberating" a hymnal to help
in selecting music. In one afternoon they typed up the program,
went to Staples to have the Mass card laminated, and found the
funeral home to handle the cremation. Michael and I sat through
one meeting in which the Catholics and the Unitarians worked
out the readings and the hymns. My mother, who had always sung
in choral groups, was vitally concerned about the music. There
was some discussion over finding someone to play the bagpipes.

My only contribution to planning the memorial was to ask for
the poem by Henry van Dyke, the one about the boat at full sail
disappearing in the distance, then coming into sight on another

shore. I had heard it read at a service not long before, and I loved
the image of a ship and the idea that the departed was not traveling alone. I needed to know that Charlotte wasn't lonely. That she
wasn't alone. I needed to know that she was feeling loved and
celebrated and that she was being held in loving arms. As much as
I was certain that death was not the end, I had no certainty at all
about the kind of existence that came after.

Meanwhile, all the mundane details of life here and now
persisted—providing meals for everyone, taking care of the
kids—and at this moment these tasks seemed utterly overwhelming. Everybody pitched in, and if they couldn't find a project on
their own, they could go see Annie, who would give them one.
Everyone seemed comforted by their busyness. I was comforted
that I did not need to entertain or be a hostess, and yet I still
couldn't settle down and just "be." This was my home, but I
couldn't find my place in it. I was not used to being the one needing comfort. I was ready to be a caretaker for the others, but that
was utterly insane, given the magnitude of my own personal loss. I
was untethered.

That's when I noticed our neighbor Livingston watching us. A
moment later he came loping over like a big, lovable dog and gave
Michael and me each a big hug that was utterly without pretense. He had a wonderfully human combination of upbeat energy
and, at the same time, an openness to life's sadness. And yet, for
me, there was an extra element of emotional safety in his not being family. He told me that I had to sit on the ground. I did, and it
was the first time I felt . . . grounded.

Michael drifted off to take care of something, and Livingston
and I sat on the grass by the stone wall in front of the forge. We
talked about how Charlotte had so quickly fallen in love with his

garden and his wife, Maggie, and Ajax, their golden retriever. They had a small pond in their yard with fairies and little secret corners and stepping-stones, and Charlotte had spent more time there than in our own yard, hopping around on the stones and throwing the ball for Ajax and admiring the fish in their pond.

"Maggie talked to the Kanebs," Liv said. They were our neighbors from down the road, an older couple who were away for the summer. They were very private, but I remembered that when we'd first moved in, Mrs. Kaneb had come by with the most wonderful chocolate cake. "They offered their house for anyone who needs a place to stay," he said. "Also the pool . . . for the kids. Keep them occupied."

We went over in the afternoon, and for the next few days Cabot and Beatrice spent most of their time in that pool with their cousins and friends.

I was relieved to see them playing happily, seemingly unaffected by the enormity of the loss. I'm not sure either of them had a true understanding of what was going on, but how could they? I was an adult and I didn't understand it at all.

Michael stayed to watch, but I slipped away and walked to the top of a nearby hill, where I sat on a bench. I could still see the house. While I wanted to be truly alone, I felt obligated to stay in touch—but at least I was far enough away that I could let down my guard and cry. Mother Nature had always been my space of healing and comfort. From my perch on the bench I looked down the hill at the large oak tree in the field and over the Kanebs' home beyond. This was the same view of the sunset that I had wanted to hold in place just days before. Now I just stared blankly and let a few tears fall. They did not come easily, but it was a start. Nobody had told me that I couldn't cry in view of the others, but nobody needed to tell me. In being stoic I was simply following through on forty years of conditioning.

I used to read gothic novels as a girl, and the image kept coming back to me of the deranged woman in a white cotton nightgown out in a rainstorm, shrieking and clawing the ground. To me, anything less than that seemed like an appalling failure to respond to what had happened. I kept wondering, "When am I going to fall off the cliff? When's it going to hit?"

And yet, even as I was feeling this chilling isolation and deep, deep discomfort, I also felt Charlotte's presence. I felt as though she were carrying me, or that I was somehow cloaked in her essence, wearing her like a blanket.

After I came back down the hill, and after the adults had returned from the pool to our house, I began drifting from room to room, asking everyone I encountered where Charlotte was. Had she reincarnated? Was she in purgatory? Was she in heaven? What was heaven? I was talking like the madwoman in some avant-garde play. I was having an existential crisis, trying to wrap my head around the loss. If I couldn't feel my way through, maybe I could think my way through.

I envied my in-laws' certainty about heaven, as well as their reliance on ritual, the comfort in prayers that were perfectly scripted and available for every occasion, mantras that kept the mind from wandering off too far into the weeds. During those first few days, Catholicism made perfect sense to me, and the more didactic and doctrinaire the better. My friends who had been raised Catholic or Jewish seemed to have an enviably solid architecture of belief, whereas we hearty Unitarians were supposed to stand alone before our God (or whatever else was up there) and figure it out for ourselves, Transcendentalist style. Confronting the cosmos head-on, with Emersonian self-reliance, alone and (supposedly) unafraid, was just something our parents assumed we would know how to do, like coming onto a mooring under sail. I was left to find my own words of comfort—except I didn't have any. I had only questions.

The church we chose for the service was just around the corner from us, where Kim had attended services as a child. She'd even been married there, and I remember the priest from when I was a bridesmaid in her wedding. His name was Father Tom Powers, and the next day he came over to help us survey the boundaries of this new territory we were entering.

With Anne and Harry as moral support, Father Tom sat us down and told us to make sure that we paid attention to any opportunities for happiness or joy or positive thoughts. He reminded us that staying steeped in pain was debilitating, and that the body could handle only so much grief before it broke down.

"It's okay to have moments when you feel okay," he said. "In fact, it's necessary."

"Great," I thought. "I'll let you know as soon as I'm tempted to feel okay."

It seemed crazy to me for anyone to suggest that we would ever feel anything other than deep and soul-searing pain. Somewhere deep down inside of me, though, his comments registered, and I would make use of them later. I knew I still had work to do in going down. Then I could worry about working my way back up.

Father Tom also told us that one of the challenges of bereavement is that we could not always rely on each other for support, because those brief windows when the sorrow seemed less burdensome would very likely not occur at the same time for each of us. We had to learn to respect where the other partner was at all times. When one of us was feeling better, we would have to work hard to not bring the other down, or to not try to force the other into the place of relief we'd found. He also reminded us that, with the death of a child, the failure rate for marriages rises to upward of 80 percent. But between Michael's Catholicism and my abandonment issues, divorce seemed an unlikely option. What seemed far more likely was simply going insane, even if we had to take turns.

Our children were the physical manifestation of our love and our devotion to each other. No one else in the world could ever represent such a deep bond for either of us. And yet I knew this was going to be tough.

When I confided in my mother that I was worried about our marriage, she asked me, "Do you want to talk to Jen and Tim?"

She meant the Yurmans, Jen and Tim, friends of the family who were therapists—a more Unitarian solution—and who had done a lot of work with grieving couples.

"Of course," I said. And it was an indication of my anxiety that I couldn't wait for them to arrive.

Mum got in touch with them and they came over, and the four of us sat outside on an old granite slab next to the forge. I can still remember the feel of the rough-surfaced granite stone in the shade of that hot day as we talked. Jen handed me rather tentatively a small ceramic angel just as we sat down. She did not say much about it other than it had caught her eye as she left her house to come visit and she thought I should have it. I was touched by the gesture and not sure how to respond. An angel? What was that about?

Tim had known both of my parents since their prep school days, and he and my dad had been great buddies at Milton Academy and at Harvard, so it was easy for me to relate to them. Obviously they were from the same world, but I'd also always admired the dash of Big Sur that they seemed to inflect into our L.L.Bean environment. As a child, I'd always thought of them as the "hippest" of my parents' contemporaries, and Tim was a big, strapping guy, a champion ski racer, not the type of therapist who wore his "sensitivity" on his sleeve. And yet their strongest credential in my book was that they had managed what looked like a very solid marriage for over fifty years.

Like any couple after fourteen years together, Michael and I had our issues, but those ordinary stresses and strains now seemed trivial in the face of what had just happened. Still, the Yurmans made it very clear that the loss of a child would be a challenge to the relationship. There would be alienation from each other and, as a couple, alienation from other couples. And yet they offered us hope. They said that with the right tools and with the right mindset, and with enough love, we might just make it through.

I remember that night, after the Yurmans had talked with us, lying in bed and being able to hear Michael's father in the kitchen talking about the death of his brothers. One had died of a brain tumor; the other had been killed in a fire at age eleven. Harry Senior had never talked about this kind of thing, so on some level it was very comforting for me to hear this opening up to sorrow among the family members down below. Hearing the sobs was more difficult.

I turned to Michael and said, "I can't imagine going through this without you."

He looked at me in the moonlight and said, "Me neither."

We made a pledge not to let this destroy us.

On the morning of Charlotte's funeral I wanted to hide in bed. I remember lying there, asking Michael all the big questions that were torturing me. Where had she gone? Was she safe? Was she happy? I was trying to appropriate some of the solid structure of his belief system to shore up my own. He was my answer man. I needed a directive.

I didn't want to see anyone, and I certainly didn't want anyone to see me. "How am I going to hold it together?" I kept asking. But that question kept alternating with "Why am I holding it together?" Either way, this was not the day to let it all hang out. This was a day to simply endure.

It was only about eight a.m. when my dear friend Sarah arrived fresh from the red-eye from San Francisco. I had flown to her side three years earlier when her son Wyatt died. Now our roles were reversed.

My mother greeted her, thanked her for coming, and immediately sent her upstairs to where we were sleeping.

She knocked softly and said, "Sukey . . . it's Sarah." I jumped up to give her a hug. For a long time we simply held each other. Then, when I stepped back to look at her, I realized that, ever the conscientious therapist, she had a fistful of handouts on grief resources, local and national.

"Don't look at these now," she said. "But you'll need them later."

Sarah was wonderfully adaptable. She could help you scrub your sink, dash off to New York with you for theater or shopping on a moment's notice, or enlighten you on the finer points of some obscure ballot proposition. She and I had met in Palo Alto and formed an immediate friendship. We were the same age and had gotten married the same year. But right now, she was the one person who could provide me with a road map based on personal experience.

Michael stood to give her a hug, and his eyes filled with tears. "Ever since I've had kids I've been afraid of this happening," he said. "Now it has. How am I going to go on?"

"You just do," she said.

We talked briefly, but I knew I had to go down to greet the others who were arriving. As I came down the stairs I saw my father and his new wife. I looked toward my mother and silently pleaded, "Mum, help me," and she took over.

I didn't mean to be callous, but I tend to take on other people's issues whether they ask me to or not, and I had already spent years trying to love my father through his drinking problems, his divorce problems, his financial problems—all the problems he pretended not to have. That day I just didn't have anything more to give.

After a quick round of hugs, Sarah and I headed back upstairs to talk. She and I processed ideas and emotions very much the same way, and I related to the fact that right out of college she'd gone to medical school and become an internist only to please her parents. She'd told me about the day she found herself in the medical closet in the hospital musing about the possibilities of self-medicating, which was the day she realized it was time to begin thinking about the career she really wanted. Shortly thereafter she began her graduate studies in psychiatry.

We'd always used each other as sounding boards without ever making judgments. I immediately launched into my questions about where Charlotte had gone and why I was having such trouble feeling my feelings. Then it struck me how many times we'd had similar talks during her own bereavement. I knew her to be a firm believer in the afterlife. Now I understood the feeling she'd expressed of a palpable, ongoing connection with her lost child.

"What am I going to do?" I kept asking.

She had already told me about how bereavement had made her a different person, altering her preferences, hobbies, even whom she chose as friends. Until her son died, Sarah had practiced psychiatry among our well-heeled community in San Francisco. After Wyatt's death, she lost interest in helping patients whose main complaint seemed to be that they had too much time on their hands. She'd taken a job as a school counselor, working with troubled teens. She'd also pulled away from the social world we'd known. I remember her telling me about being at a charity ball and trying to make polite conversation when all she wanted to do when asked "How are you?" was blurt out "My son is dead."

When I asked her why I wasn't falling apart, she reminded me of all the times she'd been like a zombie when we spent time together that first year.

"We do what we can," she said, "when we can."

I went on about the boy in the wheelchair, and about Charlotte's distress at seeing him, and how maybe that was the life that had been in store for Charlotte with her musculoskeletal issues, and that maybe this was better. Clearly I was desperate for any rationalization that could help me make sense of what had happened.

I told Sarah about Michael's idea of being chosen, as well as my sense of premonition, and she smiled. Then she described how, at the time of her own bereavement, she'd felt that she, too, had been given "special knowledge," that, maybe when she was born, God had whispered into her ear to tell her about her life this time around, and that one of the things she would experience would be the loss of a child. This resonated so powerfully with my own experience that I wondered: Do all parents simply dread the loss of a child so much that, when it happens, it seems to have been in the cards all along? And yet Michael was also furious. He had been dealt a bad hand. This was *not* in his cards.

It was a short drive to the church. As I got out of the car, I noticed that the skies looked ominous, but maybe that was just a projection of my internal state. Either way, no one had thought to bring umbrellas, and now it looked like rain.

Many of the women wore pink in honor of Charlotte. Even some of the men wore pink shirts. I wore a navy blue dress and, in honor of Charlotte, the red patent leather high heels from my closet that she had loved. We were still standing out front when a caravan of Subarus and Volvos pulled up, stopped, and began to disgorge dozens of my relatives in a sea of Forbes plaid. I had forgotten that a beloved cousin had died of a brain tumor earlier in the summer, and his service had been planned for this same day many weeks before.

Many of the Forbes men wore kilts; others limited the family tartan to their necktie. Many of the Forbes women wore it in Scottish tradition as a shoulder-to-hip sash. An outsider might have seen it as another of those peculiar WASP folkways, but to me it felt like a warm family embrace. They were showing the flag, sharing the secret handshake.

Sarah and the children and I went in and waited in a side room with the rest of the immediate family.

I leaned over and told her, "I'm still afraid I'm going to lose it."

She squeezed my hand and said, "I don't think you will, but if you do, everyone will understand."

When we stepped into the sanctuary and took our places, I found myself seated directly in front of my father. I couldn't avoid him any longer, so I turned and gave him a big hug and was saddened to feel him so diminished, aged by all his troubles well beyond his years.

The music began, and I turned to look at the crucifix with its tortured and bleeding Christ. There was nothing subtle about the Catholic iconography, so very different from the austerity of my childhood religion. I'd always yearned for the drama of those representations, and the majesty of the gold and the stained glass. As a child, I had gone to Latin Mass with my Catholic friends, and I loved losing myself in the ritual. At this moment, I could have used that sort of transport. At least there was a portrait of Mary to draw my attention away from my own pain. I had stared at hundreds of Madonnas in Italy during a junior year abroad, and I'd been inspired by the womanly strength of the Pietà, wondering how the weight of her son must have felt in her arms as she held him one last time. My arms now ached with the phantom pain amputees often report after losing limbs. Now at my own child's funeral, I found communion with this other grieving mother.

A hymn I recognized brought me out of my reverie, and it was a Protestant stalwart: "A Mighty Fortress Is Our God." This was followed by the first reading, Isaiah 25:8: "He will swallow up death in victory; and the Lord God will wipe away tears from off all faces . . ." But what are we to make of this comforting God, given that it's the same God who allows such terrible things to happen?

A young woman with a beautiful voice sang "Shepherd Me, O God," which is Psalm 23 put to music. Then Anne's father read from the Book of Revelation. This was followed by a Gospel reading for the kids, and then the Catholic prayers and the liturgy.

I thought about my sisters sitting beside me. Just a year or two earlier Heidi had suffered a major scare with melanoma. And Laura had been going through four years of hell, worrying about her son Dawson, the same age as Cabot, who suffered from acute lymphocytic leukemia. Watching my nephew suffer through chemo, and my sister with him, I had felt so guilty that I was the one being spared. I had also been better able to access the anguish over his illness than I was able to access my own anguish for now.

"How do you get through it?" I'd asked her.

"I don't have a choice," she'd said.

Father Tom began his homily, but my mind was tuning in and out. Some of the imagery was comforting, some of it far too abstract for someone as prone to questioning as I was. But then Beth got up and began to read the poem by Henry van Dyke I'd requested, and I hung on every word:

> I am standing upon the seashore.
> A ship at my side spreads her white
> sails to the morning breeze
> and starts for the blue ocean.
> She is object of beauty and strength.
> I stand and watch her until at length
> she hangs like a speck of white cloud
> just where the sea and sky come
> to mingle with each other.
> Then someone at my side says, "There, she is gone!"
> "Gone where?"
> Gone from my sight. That is all.
> She is just as large in mast and hull
> and spar as she was when she left my side

and she is just as able to bear her
load of living freight to her destined port.
Her diminished size is in me, not in her.
And just at the moment when someone
at my side says, "There, she is gone!"
There are other eyes watching her coming,
and other voices ready to take up the glad
shout: "Here she comes!"

After the reading, Father Tom stood to offer the Sacrament, but this was an even greater moment of alienation for me. The Catholic Church invites all, but it allows only those baptized in the church to participate in Communion.

Then, just as he raised his arms, a huge lightning bolt flashed, followed by a clap of thunder so close by that I felt it in my chest. For some reason the momentary lapse into the natural world was comforting to me. Was the Old Testament God of Wrath just showing off? Were the heavens opening up to rain down tears in sympathy? Or were we in some sort of Mel Brooks movie? For the briefest of moments I felt the corners of my mouth twitch into a half smile. But almost as quickly as the smile came I was jerked back into my painful reality. This was no occasion for smiles.

A deluge began to pound on the roof, and once again I thought of Charlotte, standing on the porch of Mansion House and letting the storm's water stream down on her face.

Rain or no, we still stepped outside to release helium-filled balloons as planned. Each one carried a message of love for Charlotte, written out by some loved one at the service, as well as her prayer card. For the next couple of weeks we received calls of condolence

from strangers all over the area who'd had one of these packages
descend into their yard and had been moved to reach out to us.

The storm continued to rage, and we went back inside for a
reception in the basement of the church. I saw my husband talking
to guests, milling about with three-year-old Beatrice clutched in
his arms like a security blanket. There were fluorescent lights in
the suspended ceiling, and wherever Michael went, the electrical
fixtures snapped and popped and went dark over his head.

Sarah took a late flight back to California that night, and we
dosed ourselves with Ambien and Valium once again, fearful of
waking in those grim hours well before dawn when our troubles
seemed endless and our sorrows inconsolable.

The rain continued into the day, but otherwise it was deafeningly
quiet. Most of our other guests had left or were leaving. This was
a busy time of year with school about to begin, and people needed
to get back to their lives. We were left with the immediate family,
which, given that my husband was one of six and I was one of four
and we'd produced a combined total of twenty grandchildren,
was still quite a large contingent, but not nearly enough to con-
sume all the food that was on hand. We wound up sending dishes
to the Salvation Army and flowers to hospitals and nursing homes.

Having held on through the service, I greeted this day with a
sense of relief. Now I could let it all hang out . . . if only I could
let it all hang out. Michael was even more vacant than he had been
the day before. At times it seemed as if he could barely stand up,
and he moved like someone who was ill. I did my best to comfort
him, but I was vacant and empty myself, confused and still a little
threatened by his displays of grief, which were so dramatic

compared to my own numbness. There was a growing tension between wanting to comfort my surviving children and embrace them in a present and loving way and also wanting with every fiber of my being to escape to the woods alone. In nature there has always been a comfort to the natural order—brutal as it can be. The enormity, vastness, abundance, frailty, audacity, cruelty, diversity, mysticism, raw beauty, and divine wisdom are incredibly reassuring. It is humbling. She cries out to us, "I am here for the long haul, whether or not you are. You are not that important." Somehow that knowledge of being a small piece of an awesome and connected world that was here many, many eons before us and will be here many, many eons after was reassuring to me. I know some people try in vain to tame nature. I love its raw beauty and the sheer fact that while often predictable it is not tamable. The innate chaos of nature comforts me. I have always found it especially alluring when faced with coming to grips with life and death. Life and death in their most pure form occur daily in nature. It is all around us, as is the miracle of regeneration. Growing up with four seasons was a constant reminder to me of the wondrous cycles of Mother Nature and how each was dependent upon the other.

I took my morning cup of tea out to the forge and sat there on the sofa and began to weep. It was chilly for August, and I was trying to feel Charlotte's warmth wrapped around me, but instead I experienced an excruciating wave of pain. The sky darkened—another late summer squall coming through—and then another bolt of lightning hit the lamppost just a few feet away, causing every hair on my body to stand on end. The pain dissipated, just like the clouds. I sat there, staring off into the wet green, and as the sky began to clear a doe walked by with a little fawn, just a few feet away from me. They both stopped in midstep, perfectly framed by the window, but not in the abrupt way that flight animals often freeze, then turned in tandem to stare at me. It was as if they were making eye contact with me, a mother and her young child walking together peacefully. I wanted to believe that it was a sign, like the rainbow after the storm.

Okay, here was a moment of comfort, yet I was still torn because I wanted to go with the sorrow, to really feel it, but every time I started going down, something like the doe and the fawn would catch me and pull me back up. Was Charlotte trying to protect me from the pain? I was touched, but at the same time I knew I couldn't remain insulated if I ever wanted to get through it. To get through it, I first had to really get down into it.

Later that day I ventured out into the woods, calling Charlotte's name louder and louder as if she were lost and I needed to find her. I walked along in a daze, and then I got that kicked-in-the-gut realization once more that she really was gone. I sat on a log and wailed. I repeated the process several times. Walk. Kick. Sit. Wail. My mind kept ruminating, obsessing about little mysteries like her fixation on the dead mouse and the boy in the wheelchair. And then there were the odd things she'd said over the years that were out of context. Things like, "I miss my real family." What the hell did that mean? This haunted me, especially in the sense of my own feeling that losing her had been somehow predetermined. Sometimes I felt that all of us, including Charlotte, had been merely playing roles that we might have worked out in heaven, saying, "Well, this time, you be the mother and I'll be the child," as if we'd been through this a million times before, each time exploring the different permutations of human relationship.

I realized that this perception of mine was a little nutty, and then the image came back to me of that madwoman crawling around on the lawn naked, pulling the grass up with her teeth, screaming, "Why, why, why?" I continued the scenario with the nice people from McLean coming to put me away in a padded room in a building paid for by one of my nutty ancestors. I was terrified of that happening, but at the same time was still convinced that any reaction short of utter, raving lunacy meant that I was doing it wrong. The internal monologue that informed much of my first year had begun. "If you loved her more, you would feel more." "You were overwhelmed with three children under six and you must be secretly relieved." "You are an awful mother. Just look at you—cold as ice. No feelings." The more time that passed and the less I was able to dig deep into the pain, the more strength I gave to that internal voice. It would be just a matter of time, I feared, before people saw me for what I truly was: a monster. Some terrible ugly beast incapable of human emotion, masquerading as a decent woman and going through the motions.

I'd begun to feel recrimination in Michael's eyes as well, as if he were saying, "You're not going as low as I am. That must be because you didn't love her enough." So, of course, every conflict Charlotte and I had ever experienced came back to haunt me.

Charlotte had been my most difficult baby right from the start. She had colic, and she couldn't sleep on her back or side; she slept only on her tummy or held in my arms, her face buried in my neck and her shoulders folded in like a bird mantling its wings. I've always taken pride in being upbeat, but her nature couldn't have been more different. I could ask her, "What makes you happy?" And whereas you might expect a five-year-old to say, "Sunshine! Candy! A rainbow!" she would look at me quizzically and say, "I don't know."

She didn't seem melancholy, just pessimistic, which was a real challenge for me, one that required a lot more parental imagination and energy. But her need for extra everything went hand in hand with fierce independence in thought and decision. She was born with an incisive wit and wisdom beyond her years that kept us laughing regularly with her offbeat comments. By the time she was two she had me fully sized up and could easily dress me down. As often as not, her riffing psychological assessments of me ended with an emphatic "and that's your problem, Mummy."

As much as I loved her, she wasn't easy, but all I could do now was wonder how I could ever have complained or been critical. How could I have ever done anything but relish every moment, even the moments of wrangling with her at her most difficult? Was there just not enough feeling there? Was that why I was having such a hard time feeling my feelings? Now, as I lumbered through the woods, each time my foot hit the ground I felt physical confirmation that I was here on earth . . . and that she was somewhere else.

Back at the house our guests needed a project, and they soon focused on assembling the outdoor play set we'd purchased in Palo Alto when Cabot and Charlotte were very small. We had taken it with us when we moved to Santa Cruz, then transported it to Boston. This was a guy thing, perfect for Michael and his brothers, who've always been best able to relax and relate while working with power tools. As I watched all of the Bigham boys working together physically, I was struck again by the dearth of active ritual in the early stages of grief, the kind of tasks that might help us let go. Prior to the Civil War, Michael and his brothers and probably even young Cabot would have been hand-hewing Charlotte's coffin. The physical act of that would have allowed for softer, more incremental steps toward acknowledgment of the grief. Had they made the coffin at home she would have been placed in it and then walked in a community procession of grief and support through the streets to her service and then final resting place. Before I came to experience grief firsthand, I used to view this sort of thing as very macabre. Now it took on a whole new meaning of caring and community. It allowed space for the reality of the loss to begin to take shape. Without the need to create the coffin, we were left with a void. Assembling the wooden family play structure seemed the best alternative and served at the very least to distract.

The other wives hung around to watch, but I retreated to the third floor of our house. This little garret had been selected by default as my office. There was no climate control, and only a narrow spiral afterthought of a staircase for access, but it was the only space in the house that was mine. I had my computer and files filled with family information and with personal projects, and I sat down at my desk and stared at my computer with no notion of what I was going to do except hide. Then my gaze fell upon the bulging scrapbooks I'd spent so many hours creating for the family and for each child. I'd even gone to Creative Memories workshops to get good at this sort of thing. But improving my skills had not added hours to my schedule, and so what I had, essentially, was selected piles of photographs, and announcements, postcards, brochures, and masses of kids' drawings and school reports, along with the love letters that I wrote regularly to Michael, and to each child. I plunked myself down on the floor in my own version of being brought low by grief and sitting shivah.

I flipped through the nursery school art projects and the pictures of each of them beside the gingerbread house they'd made. I had a baby book for each of the three that recorded their first

Charlotte, six, on horseback.

word, first step, and so on with all sorts of pictures and narratives. Then, from year two onward, the idea was to create a more free-form book for each of them.

Browsing through the piles, I realized that I was way ahead in organizing Charlotte's photographs and mementos. Was this part of my eerie sense of foreknowledge? After all, she was the middle child, and yet I had carried her life all the way up to age five, assembling an archive that she had delighted in looking through. But why would I be so far ahead on hers? If I had assembled her scrapbooks as I looked back, it would have been a less authentic glimpse into her short life. The first four years of her life had been documented while they were happening, and I sat for a quiet moment in gratitude for that. I had to do my best with the final two and a half years.

With Charlotte in July 2004.

I knew that this was going to be painful, like pressing on a wound to make it bleed, but I threw myself into assembling all of the rest of Charlotte's memorabilia and photos up to the present. If I truly was numb, living right now in a state of shock, then maybe this was the best time to do this work, before the full brunt of the pain hit me. But, plain and simple, it also gave me a task—something to do when I had no idea what to do. Should I be like the ancient Greeks and start reciting dirges, tear at my clothing, and beat my breasts? That fit with my gothic fears of utterly coming unglued, but it also seemed entirely out of character and therefore highly unlikely. For a while I just sat on the floor and stared blankly off at nothing in particular.

I lost myself in the photographs, browsing through the princess stories Charlotte had written in her own distinctive hand, with her own distinctive spelling. They made me cry the way you'd cry when you miss your child who was at school or camp. I simply didn't have access to the deep, gut-wrenching tears that acknowledged, "I'll never be with her again." Each of the stories she'd written and carefully bound—no matter the subject matter—ended with the same single word all alone on the last page: "Love." That was my Sweetie Pea.

One family member or another would check on me every now and then, but I must have made it clear that I wanted to be alone, because no one stayed. I organized all the recent items, then packed everything up to ship to Ann, my friend in California who had run the scrapbook workshops. I would ask her to put the final book together for me. I knew I couldn't do it myself.

At the end of the day, when I came downstairs, I was pleased to see the completed structure and all the cousins playing on it. But then the realization hit me again. Charlotte wasn't there. Where was she?

6

Naushon

We call a child who has lost her parents an orphan. An adult who loses a spouse is a widow or widower. Somehow there is no term for a parent who has lost a child, which may be because the experience was once so much the norm. Still, I don't think frequency of occurrence would have made it any easier to endure for those earlier generations of parents.

Much has been written about how the poet Emerson was tortured by the loss of his beloved son Waldo, taken by scarlet fever at the age of six. Less has been said about the grieving of the boy's mother, Lidian, who essentially took to her bed for the rest of her life, numbed by the drug of choice for nineteenth-century women, laudanum, also known as tincture of opium.

Today, even as people have easier access to their emotions, they keep their distance from the emotional reality of death, especially the death of small children. This means that a bereaved parent is treated either as a tragic figure or as a pariah. Suffering the death of a child seems almost like a curse, or freakishly bad luck, and for those who observe it, the loss brings their own vulnerability too close to home.

And yet society still seems willing to give the bereaved mother (fathers less so) a free pass. A mother who experiences this devastation could take to her bed and never emerge, and, opiates aside, I don't think anyone would blame her. That kind of understanding is a gracious gesture, I suppose, but it does nothing to really help. Not if the objective is for the mother to work through the pain and go on living.

In those early weeks my gauge for where I was in the grieving process was how long it took each morning before I got the kicked-in-the-gut wake-up call of She's Dead. Eventually, that neutral time of first awaking would move from milliseconds to minutes. But during the period when we were still sleeping on the air mattress, hearing the birds in the morning, and seeing the yellow room filled with dazzling light, I could hardly open my eyes before the rock-filled backpack dropped down onto my chest, the assigned weight I would carry around for the rest of the day.

Our house was still filled with flowers, which I'd loathed from the start. The longer they stayed, the more I found their fragrance cloying, like the smell of a disinfectant spray meant to hide something grotesque. And after that first horrible week, I hated watching them die, then having to throw them away—another acknowledgment that time was moving forward without my daughter.

A few days after the funeral, Charlotte's ashes arrived, and my first thought was "I can't believe this is all that's left of you." It wasn't just that I was holding my daughter's charred remains. It was the surreal notion that all that she had been—this huge, expansive soul, this beautiful spirit—could be reduced to fragments that would fit inside a pink cloisonné jar. My body ached and I had to hold on to something, but there was nothing to hold on to, so I just sat weeping and hugged the jar.

I knew in time I would need to go back into Charlotte's bedroom. For months it would remain off-limits for me after dark, but one bright afternoon in September I forced myself to go in. The

space had been designed as a sitting room for the master suite, and
it was on the opposite side of the house from where we were sleeping. It had a high-peaked ceiling and, with big windows on two
sides, the room was very airy. The walls were a pale blue. Charlotte's bed was an "officer's campaign" collapsible contraption
made of iron that I'd picked up from some overpriced decorator in
San Francisco just before she was born. It had four high posts that
I'd outfitted with a canopy and curtains for her. Alongside her bed,
the south window looked out over the forge. The window to the
east looked down the winding road toward the big oak tree where
I'd watched the sun go down the day she died.

On that first, tentative visit, I stood gazing at the stuffed animals on the pillows and I felt myself descending into the grief. I
lay down on Charlotte's bed as if I were going to dissolve into the
covers, and then I heard a voice say to me, "You can't do this now."

Rationally, I know it was just a thought, but I experienced it
very distinctly as hearing a voice. The voice of God? Charlotte's
voice? The voice of little green men from Mars? I don't know, but
I heard it, and it was a compelling directive. In that moment I was
keenly aware of the sensation of a succession of doors sealing
chambers inside of me. The sensation was so powerful I could almost feel the reverberations sent out as they slammed shut.

I got up and I moved over to the south-facing window, where I
noticed a nose smudge and a child's handprint on the glass. Charlotte must have been standing there looking out and holding her
face up against the windowpane. Two nights before she died we'd
sent her to her room for teasing her sister. I pictured her in that
spot staring out at us in the yard while she did penance. My gut
ached at the thought of her missing out on the few precious moments she had left. I put my hand on that spot as close as possible

without touching it and put my cheek up against it the same way. I would not let anyone clean that window for years.

In her room there were built-in bookcases with cabinets below that we'd turned into closets. The shelves were lined with animals and dolls, and pottery and artwork she'd done at school. There were also framed black-and-white photographs of each of the children. On the floor was a horse corral the size of a dollhouse. It was all so perfect. Too perfect. We'd only just moved in and she hadn't even had time to get it messy.

Desperate to occupy my mind, and ever the frugal Yankee, I began to organize her clothes and wrap them up, with hand-me-downs in mind. Her baby blanket, the towels with her name, her favorite pink sweater, the pineapple dress she wore around her waist like a long gypsy skirt. On one of the shelves was a pair of sparkly, sequined Mary Janes, and inside of them I could see the small dark depressions of her individual toes where the material had conformed to her foot. I put these on my dresser. Everything else I stored in a box, which I methodically labeled for future use, "Charlotte. Age six to eight."

In the weeks ahead, whenever I was especially sad, I would go up and rummage through that box. One afternoon I clutched the pink sweater to my face and I almost fell over. I'd never thought that Charlotte had a distinctive smell until I recognized it. It was the smell of fresh air. But there was also the slight sweetness of newly mown hay, and maybe a hint of sea spray. It occurred to me that the last time she'd worn this sweater was on Naushon. This was the scent of a child who'd been running around and getting sweaty beneath a layer of sunscreen. Next thing I knew my knees had given out and I was on the floor sobbing, without inhibition, without the least bit of self-consciousness. The crying, of course, was an incredibly welcome physical release, but the mere fact that I was able to cry was every bit as powerful. "I can do this," I thought. "I'm human after all."

From then on I cried every day. I put the sweater in a ziplock bag, and each afternoon I'd go up and open it and sniff it, and for a long time it smelled like her. With so much opening and closing, though, the smell began to fade. After a while it just smelled like a plastic bag.

Michael and I continued to need pills in order to sleep; I found everything more miserable in the dark hours between midnight and four a.m. Images of Charlotte's last hours and the internal dialogue of my personal failings as a mother, wife, caretaker would make falling back asleep impossible and the sleep deprivation would make it all worse the next day as well. I took Ambien to avoid being awake at that time, but there are limits to how much of that stuff one can take.

One morning I found my husband sitting in the living room staring off into space. I had to get the kids off to school, but when I came back a half hour later he hadn't moved.

"Are you okay?" I asked.

"I don't know," he said. He seemed catatonic.

I decided to stay there with him, sitting quietly. After a while I asked again, "Are you okay?"

"I don't know," he repeated, but it was clear he couldn't get out of the chair. "Something's not right."

That same night I was awakened by the most horrible sound out on the porch. I found my husband outside in his pajamas screaming in a shrill, keening way that seemed completely out of character. I could see him lit in profile by the light coming from inside the house. I sat down on the stone steps, hugged my knees, and wrapped my nightgown tightly around my legs. He was roiling in such anger that I was scared to go too near, but I was also worried about him. Then, as I watched, he picked up one of the huge granite planters sitting by the door and hurled it across the lawn. My gothic nightmare of derangement was coming true— only it wasn't happening to me. It was Michael who was headed down the Charlotte Brontë path, and there wasn't room for both of us. Rather than turning me into the mad wife in the attic from *Jane Eyre*, grief was turning Michael into the brooding Rochester.

Maybe his Catholic faith was too abstract, or his idea of heaven and the afterlife too distant, to provide anything more than momentary comfort. When scientists ask people to describe their concept of God, most respondents come up with some vague projection of themselves, only with supernatural powers. That same inchoate drive to extend the ego permeates so many attempts to prolong life, or defeat death. Some people leave instructions for their head to be removed and stored in liquid nitrogen in hopes of physical resurrection. Technical types talk about downloading the full contents of human brains onto hard drives that—theoretically—could last forever. But does a record of all your experiences, combined with every factoid that ever registered in your frontal lobes, constitute *you*? I don't think so.

In those early days I began to search for books that might encourage me, or even guide me through this period of intense question, doubt, and misery. Most of what I read was that life was going to be forever changed (a pretty obvious insight, that one), but that if I was really lucky, at some point in the distant future I might find a "new normal." The implication was that the best I could hope for was to go on living, but in an attenuated sort of way. And then, eventually, I'd be dead, too, so no worries.

That's not what I wanted. I was determined to embrace my grief and devastation fully, and then to come out fully on the other side. But at this point in time, the priority was to hold the family together. If anyone was going to do it, for now it looked as though it was going to have to be me.

Michael's parents had stayed on to look after us. They were retired, with time on their hands, but they were also genuinely worried about us, and they certainly wanted to help, especially with the kids. We had just moved into this new house and there were a million small errands to run, especially with back-to-school shopping upon us, so it was quite a comfort to have them around, though neither is the kind of person you can sit down with and have a good cry. Then again, I had the opposite problem. I had the feeling that they might be judging me for not being emotional enough. After all, their son was crying all the time.

As we tried to formulate our survival plan, my first thought was that we had to get back to Naushon. In part this was a matter of getting back on the horse that had thrown us. We had been on the island just before Charlotte's death, and I didn't want to have a place so sacred to me tainted with those sad associations. But more than that, Naushon had always been the place where life had made the most sense. The palpable presence of ancestors. The soothing of natural rhythms. The structure was so solid and secure that you went with it without question. You didn't have to do anything. It was enough to simply be.

We drove down on a Thursday, the four of us plus Michael's parents, and even on the ride to Woods Hole I found comfort in the familiarity of the route. But then a new anxiety began to take over. Everything about our life in suburban Weston was new to us, so there was no well-established fabric from which Charlotte would be absent. Today would be our first exposure to otherwise familiar family experiences with my daughter written out of the script.

The small gravel lot for the Naushon ferry is next door to the restaurant that was the scene of our last outing together. We pulled in and parked, and everyone piled out of the car and wandered over to the adjacent ice-cream parlor. Instead of joining them, I took a moment to go over to the restaurant and step inside. I stood just inside the door, scanning the scene of vacation travelers eating seafood, then stepped back outside. I knew I had to confront certain things now in order to avoid land mines later. I could check the Landfall off the list.

Returning to the parking lot, I helped Michael and his parents with the bags and the kids. Fortunately, on that day, on that boat, the only other passengers were guests we didn't know, so we were able to remain insulated and anonymous a little longer. Then, too, I had seen most of the family at Charlotte's service, but I still dreaded the awkwardness of those first encounters with people who would have to tell us how sorry they were.

The ferry itself is fifty-six feet, with a wheelhouse for passengers and a freight deck that can accommodate two pickups or one long oil truck. The ride is all of fifteen minutes—twenty if you stop at Uncatena—but each time the captain backs away from the dock and turns hard to starboard I always have the exalted feeling of embarking on a great journey. That's the magic of islands. The smell of the sea air assaults your senses and the tension fades from your body the instant you leave the mainland.

Catholics have the stations of the cross and their rosaries. I've always had the ritual of leaving Woods Hole and heading out past the ledges, past Penzance Point, with all its fabulous houses and the terra-cotta-roofed Mellon estate—the same route each time. It's a complicated waterway, one primary east-to-west passage with a fork that runs southeast, but, barring serious fog, you can see your destination the whole time. Then there's a quarter mile of open water and then another set of ledges marking the outer part of Hadley Harbor, and all along there are familiar channel markers, nuns and cans and spindles with birds and sometimes dolphins and seals. This was, of course, the setting for my nightmare in which Charlotte slipped away from me in the current, but I couldn't let that torture me now. I had enough images tormenting me as it was.

We stood on the railing, Cabot and Beatrice in their life jackets, looking out to where the horses were grazing on Nonamesset. Then we went through the narrows and I could see the red boathouse and the big stone house with a large widow's walk on the hill, a sight I never grow tired of seeing. I was home.

As soon as we stepped off onto the dock, we transferred our bags and our groceries to a garden cart. Then, with Michael as our draft animal pulling the load, we walked together alongside the meadow on the trail leading up to Mansion House.

I was filled with trepidation as I saw the large copper birch tree with the rope swings, the split-rail fence, the sundial. Then I looked across the porch and saw Charlotte standing there in the rain. That image, too, I forced out of my mind.

We climbed the steps and opened the front door, and immediately on the front hall table I found a gift left for me by one of my cousins. It was a photo of a double rainbow stretched from one end of the island to the other. She had glued it to a piece of driftwood decorated with seashells and glass, with a note explaining that the picture had been taken on August 18—the day Charlotte died.

We unpacked and had some lunch, and then Michael and I left the grandparents to babysit and walked together to the Aisle of Beeches, where the family memorials are. In this quiet spot in the middle of a beech forest there are also several actual graves, including those of William and Lydia Swain. They were the aunt and uncle who had taken in their niece Sarah Hathaway, who later married John Murray Forbes. JMF and William Swain were also business associates, and until just prior to William's death, the two families had owned Naushon jointly. John Murray Forbes and Sarah Swain Hathaway Forbes named their eldest son, my great-great-grandfather, William in honor of William Swain.

We stood for a moment, looking up the rise toward the spot we'd already picked out for our family memorials. As usual, there were bright shafts of light shining down through the shade of the beeches.

"We were supposed to be here first," I said to Michael. Then I walked up the rise and, like a gothic heroine, fell down sobbing, clutching the largest boulder. A few weeks later we would transform that hunk of granite into Charlotte's memorial.

Michael stayed with me until my tears had passed, but eventually he said he wanted to get back to the house. I let him go, but I felt the need for one of the long, solitary walks I'd taken on the island all my life.

Naushon is actually a series of islands—Monahansett, Uncatena, Naushon, Veckatimest, Nonamesset—connected by footbridges. Ice Age glaciers had formed them by scraping debris into a long ridge known as a terminal moraine that extends into Buzzards Bay on a southwest heading of sixty degrees. Hills rise up to

Our family together in summer 2004.

two hundred feet, often topped with sand, but also mixed with huge boulders of granite and gneiss. This landscape is punctuated by "kettle holes," formed when big chunks of ice hung around and displaced the rock that otherwise would have settled in. Some of these deep impressions became ponds.

I walked through the woods and out toward the south shore. I walked past the owl's nest high up in the beech tree in the woods. I came up the hill to the main road, then crossed onto Eagle Hollow path and walked back along the north shore.

I walked along the path that took me past the collection of boulders that had been a ceremonial circle for the Wampanoags long before our family's tenure on the island. I knew very little about the beliefs of these Native Americans, but I did know that their religion (like mine) encompassed both the natural and the supernatural worlds, and that it was very much grounded in a sense of place—this place. I had done so much living here. I always felt so alive here. Now I felt utterly numb, bereft, and diminished. What was I going to do? The choices seemed basic and slim: Die. Exist. Live. I wanted to die, but with two young children to care for and a husband, that wasn't an option. Exist. I could do that. I was doing that now. But how flat and lifeless. How dreary and endless the long march would be until I met Charlotte again. The only option that resonated with me was to live. But how? How to get there from here? To feel the fullness of life again seemed a Sisyphean task and yet I knew that somehow I had to get there. I would do whatever it took. And when I got there, I would reflect on it and hopefully help others behind me on the path. *I wanted to want to live.* That was the best I could do in that moment. I decided step one would be to fake it until I could make it.

Every now and then I found myself kicking the ground just to remind myself that I was alive. I was also literally connecting with the earth, perhaps on Charlotte's behalf as well. She was no longer physically present, so I would engage the natural world for both of us. I noticed as the footing changed from grass to leaves to sand to stone to well-worn dirt roads with grass in the center. I focused on the change in the sound as I kicked the different surfaces.

The first bridge is over the lagoon, also called the Southeast Gutter, which offers a very different experience depending on whether the four-foot tide is high or low, coming or going. Just two weeks earlier Charlotte and I had been swimming here, jumping off the bridge to ride the tide surging beneath as it rushed out to sea. How can this be, I wondered? How can the world change so suddenly, so absolutely, so irrevocably?

Emerson had walked these same paths, and he had mused over similar mysteries, and, like me, he had not found it easy to emote. "I chiefly grieve that I cannot grieve," he wrote after the death of his son. "I comprehend nothing of this fact but its bitterness. Explanations I have none, consolation none that rises out of the fact itself; only diversion, only oblivion of this and pursuit of new objects." Yes, I thought. But help me. Fix me. You who were here before. Help me.

I came into the pasture where I'd seen the apparition emerge from the lightning bolt so long ago. I lay down on the grass, facedown, taking Livingston's advice about being grounded one step further. Emerson said that the use of natural history is to give us aid in supernatural history. He also said that the outer creation was to give us the language for the inward creation. Surely I was every bit as desperate as he had been for some deeper understanding of the incredible rupture that had taken place in my life. If I couldn't make sense of it through logic, I was willing to try osmosis, photosynthesis—anything. If it would help me break through the numbness and embrace the pain and truly feel it and then get beyond it, I was ready to worship thunder and pray to trees.

The trouble remained—I was a religious community of one, without sufficient teaching or ritual to fall back on. I needed a spirit guide, and I had no idea where to find one.

After a time I got up and continued my walk, then went back to check on Cabot and Beatrice. When I got to the house I found Michael sitting on the porch with a yellow legal pad, his father a few feet away in a rocker, two generations grieving together.

"What're you doing?" I asked.

He showed me the drawing on the pad.

"For Charlotte," he said.

It was a design for a playhouse, surrounded by formal plantings. There had once been a stable between Mansion House and the meadow that now served as a soccer field. Michael had mentioned in passing that he wanted to build a memorial garden there for Charlotte. Now he seemed deeply into it.

"Nothing that needs a lot of maintenance," he said. "We have to keep it simple. After we're gone it can't fall into neglect and become a jungle."

He was being wise to plan ahead. At Stone House, Emerson's daughter Edith had built a circular garden, enclosed by a high stone wall and accessed by an iron gate. Five generations later it had gone from lovingly tended to a tangle of weeds that was now almost impossible to enter. As children, we pretended that it was *the* Secret Garden, à la Frances Hodgson Burnett.

I touched Michael's shoulder, and then, as I stepped toward the door, I noted the look on Harry Senior's face. He was sitting very still, observing with silent, fatherly concern. The two of them spent most of the afternoon in that same spot: Michael drawing on his pad, and Harry watching.

Betty and my mother had the kids under control, so I went into the parlor and sat down with one of the guest books I'd brought down to the island to read. These ancient ledgers were made for keeping accounts, bound in leather with "Naushon" embossed in gold leaf on the front.

Each house on the island has its own set, but given that Mansion House's guest books go back to 1837, we keep them in archival condition in acid-free boxes fastidiously stored off-site, along with other climate-sensitive family papers.

For nearly two centuries the benchmarks in family history had been collected here. Reading the entries in old faded script has always been a rainy-day activity for me. And given the cast of characters who've passed through, there are treasures to be found, most with a summery, magical feel. Herman Melville's was typical in that regard:

July 13, 1852

Sweet shall be the memory of Naushon.

Blue sky—blue sea—& almost everything blue but our spirits.

Herman Melville's signature and note in the Mansion House guest book.

There were also autumn entries of deer-hunting parties. Guests like Emerson and Oliver Wendell Holmes would compose poems to recite at the evening's formal hunt dinners and then write them in the book for future reference.

But this day I wasn't browsing for literary footnotes. I was desperately seeking guidance from my ancestors about life, and death, and grieving, and the meaning of it all.

Knowing that the American Civil War had been a time of great loss and anxiety, I began to look through the pages of a volume that held entries from these dates. Fairly quickly my eyes fell on the familiar and practically indecipherable handwriting of my great-great-great-grandfather Ralph Waldo Emerson. The entry was a poem he had written during his visit on the island. The title, "Waldeinsamkeit," I later learned, refers to the process of transcending the individual self to find a healthy relationship with the universal spiritual dimension arrived at generally through solitude in the forest and meditation. The word *Einsamkeit*, without the *Wald* in front of it, describes one who is locked inside oneself and is thus driven mad. I feared I was the latter but hoped to one day have the ability to become the former. It took quite some time to painstakingly transcribe the words in ink, but I was determined to make it through the poem in its entirety. Reading the first stanza was the closest I had come to an "aha" moment with my grandfather Emerson's writings:

> I do not count the hours I spend
> In wandering by the sea.
> The forest is my loyal friend,
> Like God it useth me.

There were also collections of letters, including one from great-great-grandfather William Hathaway Forbes himself, the former prisoner of the Civil War, about the death of his own son Don, whose appendix had ruptured on this island on his eighteenth birthday. Though he died almost a hundred years prior to my birth, I knew this young man's features as well as my own because I've been drawing my fingers across the smooth plaster cheekbones of his death mask in the attic since I was a child.

"Yes, these are sad anniversaries," William Hathaway Forbes

not believe that our loved ones perish but that they
· life, and our hope is inextinguishable that we shall
····· ···· again."

The summer that Don died, his mother, Edith Emerson, wrote about going up to the "fort" he'd built on what's now called Don's Hill. She tells of filling his room with flowers and candles each year on the anniversary of his death, which, of course, was also the anniversary of his birth.

But, as moving as these documents were, the most haunting account I found was written by Sarah Forbes's cousin Robert Swain, the man whose death allowed Naushon to pass entirely into Forbes family ownership. It reminded me of a letter I'd just received from friends in California telling me about a near-death experience. A friend of theirs, Rod, had nearly died, and he found the glimpse of the afterlife so appealing, they said, that he didn't want to come back. He was positively annoyed that he had come back. He wrote about it extensively and in fact made it his life's work to share the experience.

Robert Swain's death at twenty-two had been one of the classic romantic tubercular episodes of that era. He had suffered much, through many trips to warmer climates, with a stiff upper lip and many sentiments expressed throughout. Supposedly his last words were: "I go to join our dear friends who have gone before me, and they are not a few. We shall meet again in a better world."

But a week before the end, just before his tuberculosis took a critical turn, he wrote this:

At one time, during this last attack of hemorrhage, I felt that I was dying. Everything grew dim before my eyes. My memory failed me. I could not think of the next word I wished to say, and I could not utter the one upon my lips. A delightful feeling of peace, of freedom from all pain and suffering, of withdrawal from the world, came over me. My mind was perfectly clear. I had no thought of returning to life! This, then, is death, and now, I thought, nothing but the last rattle in the throat is wanting before my spirit takes its flight. And I *listened* to hear it. The thoughts, the feelings of that one instant of time were such as could not be in any other instant in life. The change, the great change, *now is*. With what an agony of expectation, of hope, of wonder, did my mind turn upon itself, to feel its own change, to follow out, as it were, its own identity, through the changes it was to pass through. This was all over in one instant. By the last efforts of nature, a cough threw the blood from my lungs, and I revived again. It was very painful to return to so much suffering, and the sensation was of unmingled regret.

Robert's story, coupled with Rod's, laid the foundation for a new path for me. I was intrigued by their intimations of an afterlife, and comforted by the bliss they found in their glimpses of it.

As the weekend came on, more people showed, and I had the pleasant sensation of being embraced by the clan. I held to the family tradition, playing the part dry eyed and stoic, and yet I continued to feel the same wrenching divide: relieved that I wasn't coming unglued, tortured for not coming unglued.

A central tenet of the Forbes guide to life is that, no matter what, the summer's activities should go on. Staying busy, like "staying cheerful," may be an effective way of "managing" unruly emotion, but it's a woefully inadequate response to grief.

This particular Saturday afternoon had been set aside for the annual games on horseback that went by the fancy colonial British name Gymkhana. For decades, the idea has been to engage everyone—all ages and abilities—in relay races, pattern races, whatever anyone could think up. The entry-level event is Red Light/Green Light, which the youngest rider is always allowed to win. Cabot was in the Egg and Spoon Race, the next level up, in which contestants ride in a circle, reverse, trot and cantor, all while holding an egg in a spoon. The egg falls—you're out. He was also in an event in which a team of riders has to cantor, reverse, and so on while not breaking a ribbon of toilet paper strung between them. There were relay races—four riders on a team, one horse per team—and Musical Sacks, in which contestants rode in a circle to the accompaniment of my cousin Irving on the bassoon. When the music stopped, the riders had to dismount and jump onto one of the diminishing number of grain sacks distributed around the ring.

I sat on the sidelines from start to finish, watching with a frozen, disconnected smile. Whenever I could see that I was supposed to cheer, the effort was so forced that I felt as if my internal organs were being ripped apart.

Michael remained the more stereotypically grief-stricken parent, always visibly shaken, moving like a zombie, staring silently. I was very aware of how shattered he looked, but also relieved that no one seemed to be judging him. Of course, that left plenty of room for me to feel that they were judging me.

Toward the end of the day, Cabot and Beatrice joined in the big, all-ages soccer game in the pasture near our house, so once again we did our part and were there for them on the sidelines. But the evening's entertainment—a sing-along over at Shore House hosted by my aunts—I knew was going to be just too much for me.

After dinner Michael took the kids; I stayed at Mansion House and went up on the roof, where a trapdoor leads out onto an old platform that had once been a proper widow's walk. I've always liked to go up there in the morning with a cup of tea, or sometimes in the evening with a glass of wine. On the Fourth of July there's often a gang of us perched up on the ridge, watching fourteen different fireworks displays from Rhode Island to Hyannis to Martha's Vineyard.

The footing is a little treacherous, but given my state of mind at this moment I wasn't particularly worried about personal safety. You unfasten a rusty eye hook to remove the hatch; then you climb up the ladder and you're out in the open with an unobstructed view in all directions. To the south I could see down the hill and through the beech forest to the Vineyard. To the east the view extended over the pasture and the harbor toward Penzance Point and Woods Hole. To the north was the Mansion House meadow, the farmhouse, and the stable, and then the widow's walk of Stone House. Another quarter turn and I could see all the way across Buzzards Bay to Dartmouth and the lights of Padanaram.

That night, I was still so fearful of the numbness that I relished my ability to simply drink in the sounds of the bugs and the birds and smell of the ocean. I had so many things on my mind—worries about our marriage, worries about the kids—that I tried to blot everything out and just not think. The wind had come around and I could hear the halyards clinking against the masts in the harbor, hear the sheep rustling around in their pens, the horses in the pasture. What I couldn't bear to hear was the southwest wind carrying the singing over from Shore House. I could handle the voices coming together in harmony and singing rounds like "Dona Nobis

Pacem," but it was a silly one, "The Cat Came Back," that really got to me. It had been Charlotte's favorite.

The next morning I got up early and went on a rampage cleaning closets, trying to organize things that had resisted organization for half a century. The linen closet was a real archaeology project, with moth-eaten sheets and tablecloths embroidered with my great-great-great-grandmother's initials, and spoons with handles engraved with a single "F," and a tatami mat from when my great-great-uncle Cam was ambassador to Japan. I packed up close to fifty mismatched teacups and saucers and even more crystal of various types along with stacks upon stacks of china from the China trade. Most were chipped beyond their ability to be useful or even decorative, but no one had dared get rid of them. Given the number of "aunties" who could always drop by to inquire about a missing this or that, getting rid of anything could be problematic. So all the things I wanted to deep-six I simply labeled and put in the cellar.

While conducting these excavations, I couldn't help thinking about this strange world that had made me who I am. There was so much I loved about my family, and yet I also knew that my family was the source of the emotional restraint that was just now holding me in a hellish limbo. The reluctance, perhaps inability, to express emotion had been woven into every cell in my being. But for all the focus on tradition, was there really nothing in all that family history that could actually help me find my way?

In my parents' world, strong emotions suggested weakness, and even a too easy smile was considered flaky. "Californians show their teeth too much," my father told me once. Part of that disdain is habit, part a cultivated Brahmin style, and some a reasonable response to face-freezing New England winters. But I suspect it also harbors a deeply entrenched fear. The passions are biological, after all, and we all know where biology leads.

To this day, I have never heard either of my parents raise their voices to anyone, or use foul language. When we were children, any lively expressions of emotion on our parts were met with a drawn face, tight lips pursed in a line, lowered chin, elevated eyes staring right at us. In Milton, if we were overexuberant we would be sent outside to run laps around the house three times. The message: Come back when you can hold yourself together.

The same tight reins held for any other desire, including ambition, and yet there were also the high demands that follow from that adage "To whom much is given, much is expected." It was as if we were supposed to have been born with the effortless ability to write Latin and speak French and possibly a bit of German, play a musical instrument, sing, be a quick wit with a sarcastic sense of humor, have strong opinions on a variety of issues and always defend them in a calm and well-articulated argument, and put ourselves last while always playing as a team. "I need" and "I want" were never to be spoken. It was simply not important what you needed or wanted. It was the vast indifference of nature on a smaller scale. It's not the individual that counts. It's the family that will live on, the tradition.

We were supposed to be slim and physically fit, not from vulgar exercise at a gym, but from tennis, horseback riding, gardening, polo, clearing trails, or hauling in the mainsheet. But for me, there was always a disconnect as to how one was supposed to learn how to do any of these things, because if you did them poorly you would be met with that pained and withering look of disapproval, pity, shame.

This emotional stiffness was mingled with a perplexing spiritual fluidity, which was, I guess, par for the course set by Emerson's elevation of self-reliance to the apotheosis of virtues, and nature as the text for every lesson worth learning. "The foregoing generations beheld God and Nature face to face," he wrote. "We, through their eyes. Why should not we also enjoy an original relation to the universe?"

If there was any place where Emerson's idealization of nature made sense, it was this island, which was even more "supernaturally" idyllic when I was a child. In those days, one of the caretakers would always come down to meet the boat with a team of Clydesdales—Samson and Delila—to carry up the luggage. Everyone had their own horses then, and riders would come down to greet their guests as well. The sound of hoofs on the dock is one of those rich, embedded memories from early childhood, like the smell of those Hudson Bay blankets or the Gilbey's jug filled with water, then warmed at the hearth to warm my bed.

But summering on Naushon and being to this particular manner born also meant a lot of what we called "CB," for "character building." It began with spring work details to help to open up the houses, launch floats and boats and docks, split wood, and clear trails with a chain saw. "We will walk on our own feet," Emerson wrote. "We will work with our own hands."

At one time these chores also involved managing more than a thousand sheep that roamed the meadows all summer. In the spring and fall, every family member over the age of ten would go out "sheeping" to help drive the flock to the east end of the island to be penned and sheared and cared for. The sheep that managed to stay out would become known as "woolies" because their coats just kept growing. After the roundup each year there was usually a campfire on the beach and a big sing-along. But then the coyotes took over in the eighties, and now there are only about fifty sheep on hand, kept mostly as lawn ornaments.

In my youth, it was my grandfather David who was the straw boss in all this. "A good worker" was his highest compliment. Although we had one of the oldest phone systems in the United States, the phones were rarely used. The exception was the Saturday morning phone calls we would get dragooning all on hand for a clearing party up island. We cousins would jockey to avoid answering, because whoever picked up would be in charge of rounding up the crew to meet at the farm with loppers, saws, and pruners for the long, hot tractor ride to the work site. These work details would run all morning and end on the beach with a skinny dip led by my grandfather, and then a small lunch of fruit, eggs, and cheese.

If we were staying in my grandfather's house, we would wake to a single knock on our bedroom door at seven a.m. We were expected to be in the dining room for a formal breakfast at seven thirty a.m. on the dot and would be given our marching orders then. One did not miss meals at my grandfather's house, where he would hold court and sit at the head of the long mahogany table. At the far end was a fireplace with a floor-to-ceiling wooden surround, ornately carved, and on the other three paneled walls hung large oil paintings in gilt plaster frames in various stages of disrepair. Breakfast for three or four would feel rather lonely at a table that regularly seated twenty-two at dinner.

We always showed up for meals out of respect, but also because the portions were so small we would never miss an opportunity to eat, and we were never allowed in the kitchen.

After my grandfather's death, one of his cooks shared with me her concerns about routinely being asked to serve a one-pound roast for a group of six. Potatoes and cookies were always cut in half for better sharing.

We children knew that anytime we were fortunate enough to get an invitation to stay at Mansion House with Grandfather, we needed to bring granola bars as emergency rations.

Playtime was intricately woven into work time with my grandfather, but being seen as lazy was a surefire way of being dismissed, seemingly forever. And yet the censure and the praise were equally subdued.

I remember once when I was about twelve, sailing with him on *Ariel*, his thirty-foot sloop. We were heading upwind and he asked me to trim the sail. I was a bit stunned, but also honored, and the combination must have brought all my preadolescent klutziness to the surface. I put the fine mahogany and brass handle in the winch and began to crank, and somehow that beautiful handle went flying out of my hand and into the depths of Buzzards Bay. For a moment time stood still. My brother Jamie was on board, and I could read the message on his face loud and clear: You are such an idiot and you are *so* dead.

After a protracted silence, my grandfather leaned toward me and said, "Suzannah, did you just drop my winch handle overboard?"

I winced, closed my eyes, and tried to disappear. "Yes, Grandfather, I did."

"Well," he said, "I'd very much prefer that you not do that again."

I had feared that this would be the end of our relationship, but it may have been the beginning. In that moment I knew he loved me, and afterward there was a closeness, as if we'd understood: And this will be our little secret.

Naturally, all that rectitude and forbearance was not without cost. When you squeeze the human spirit in one place you often get a bulge in another, which in the Forbes family meant even more eccentricities, like this same austere grandfather's fondness for sailing nude, for leading us all on multigenerational skinny dips throughout my childhood, and for giving his granddaughters shotguns as debutante presents.

For all of us, Grandfather included, Naushon was our one escape from emotional collars buttoned way too tight. A Naushon summer included the freedom to be a rebellious teen without doing any damage. It's a Forbes rite of passage to be brought home in a wheelbarrow by your cousins after drinking too much beer in the woods. Those were the kinds of memories I'd wanted Charlotte to have. (Well, perhaps not as a passenger in the wheelbarrow.)

In trying to assimilate these divergent family traditions I was like that Steve Martin character having a fistfight with himself.

As I look back now at the note I left in the guest book just two weeks after Charlotte's death, I find something chilling in my peculiarly WASP detachment:

August 22–30

It has been a memorable summer. We relocated the Bigham home (from Woodside, California, to Weston, Massachusetts) in June and then had an idyllic month of July here at Mansion House. We had a lovely early August weekend on Nashawena with the Miller family (Jacki Forbes's daughter Nicole) and then a wonderful stormy weekend for Shareholders here with the whole crew. Friday night's potluck is fast becoming a tradition and gets better each year.

Our late August has been hit with enormous sorrow as our beloved middle child, Charlotte Saltonstall Bigham, died suddenly and unexpectedly at age 6½. We believe the cause was spontaneous malignant hyperthermia made worse by a possible underlying neuromuscular condition. We are all still reeling from this loss but are comforted by the family support we have felt from everyone. It is our hope to create a memorial garden here in her name. Charlotte will be deeply missed and always remembered.

Sukey and Michael,
Cabot and Beatrice.

Following the entry, seven-year-old Cabot drew a small figure of a little girl and wrote "Charlotte" underneath it.

For years, leaving Naushon meant standing on the bow of the ferry with the wind in my face, looking toward Woods Hole. This time I had to stand on the stern looking back. I felt as though I was being ripped away from my mother's breast, and I just could not stop the tears. I could have hidden on the island forever, huddled in this small, secure, and limited world where the rules were clear, and where we'd already had the confrontations with our sorrow and made the adjustments. God only knew what life was going to demand of us back in the real world.

We still had two children to take care of, and Michael had a demanding job, so we tried to gear back in as August drew to a close and "back to school" required more and more of my attention.

Gifts of food were continuing to arrive, which we appreciated, but which created their own kind of stress. My friends from Dana Hall had set up one system, and then the room parents from our new school, Meadowbrook, started another. The meal was supposed to arrive by six, but somehow at the last minute I'd always be anxious about its arrival. Often something was missing, or we'd have to cook it further, which seems so simple in retrospect, but at the time anything beyond pulling off aluminum foil and portioning onto plates was too much for me. At least a few times by accident or schedule glitch no meal showed up at all, which increased the anxiety. The meal delivery was an extremely generous and kind gesture from the community but I was almost relieved when it stopped.

We ate very little after Charlotte's death anyway. We also made a rule that we should not drink any alcohol, so Michael and I both lost weight. Then I started jogging every day, not because I cared about being fit—I just needed to do something. And I needed to wear myself out so I could sleep.

The community was very careful with us, but I still dreaded seeing anyone—more of those "initial encounters" after the loss of a child. We were the new couple in town, and we'd just lost a child, which everyone knew because of a letter the headmaster at the children's new school sent around to all of the families attending the school. Of course, Charlotte's death was the first thing to come up in conversation, and I found myself being forced to comfort these new friends and neighbors. I wanted to work through the entire population of Weston right away so that all the people who needed to tell me how sorry they were could just get it over with.

Parents' night at school arrived, and sitting in the classroom felt like a hallucination. All the other mothers were talking about reading and math skills and I was wondering where Charlotte was. Heaven? Hell? Purgatory? The void? I just didn't know.

As we struggled to return to "ordinary life," I didn't want Beatrice or Cabot to become resentful or jealous of their dead sister, so I tried hard not to make a shrine of her room. I also made it clear that they were free to play with Charlotte's toys. As often as not, going into Charlotte's room, Beatrice would say to me, "Charlotte's in here. She's hiding . . . but she's in here." I wanted to believe it so much that I'd play along. I was working on rational coping mechanisms, but irrational was definitely gaining ground.

On September 21, on a new moon tide, a great white shark swam into the lagoon on Naushon and was stuck there for ten days. This was a fourteen-foot female circling around in Charlotte's favorite swimming hole, the place where we'd jumped from the bridge to get shushed along by the tide. This time there wasn't the slightest doubt—Charlotte was sending me a message.

I pulled the kids out of school and we drove down and got on the ferry with the news helicopters overhead and reporters swarming onto the beaches from small boats. They were trespassing, crowding onto the far side of the lagoon, but I didn't care. The fact that this shark was getting international attention simply confirmed the importance I assigned to it. I waded out and stood on a rock in the lagoon with this great white swimming four feet away. I was completely mesmerized, oblivious to the danger, snapping pictures and gasping in awe each time it circled past. It wasn't until I had the film developed that I really saw the giant eye looking right at me.

Had I come unglued? Lost my mind? For Melville's Ahab, it was the "whiteness of the whale" that most horrified him. But for me, I saw even this fierce creature through Emersonian eyes.

The rock where I was perched was a rock that Charlotte and I had jumped off of, laughing and splashing as we entered the then safe waters only a few weeks prior. But now this representative of the wild, uncharted territories was trapped right here, unable to get back to where she belonged. Was Charlotte going through something similar in a parallel universe? The marine biologists on site calmed the shark and tagged her with a monitor and nurtured her until they could coax her out of the lagoon and through the small channel back out into the open water. Two days after she found her freedom, she managed to dislodge her tracking device and it floated to the surface. Maybe this magnificent animal just didn't want to submit to rational study or even detailed observation. Maybe she preferred to remain a mystery, fading back into her natural environment.

7

Snow Falling Faintly

In ancient times the autumnal equinox was thought to be when the physical and the spiritual worlds were most closely aligned. As the days shortened and the nights drew long, the Celts, for one, imagined the souls of the dead coming back to mingle with the living, so they built bonfires in their honor, but, somewhat conflicted, they also wore masks to hide from any spirits who might bear a grudge. Eventually, the church co-opted this celebration and turned it into All Hallows' Eve, which American marketers co-opted and refocused on children's love of dressing up and eating candy.

With October drawing to a close, Cabot and Beatrice, like grade schoolers everywhere, wanted to spend All Hallows' Eve trick or treating, so we took them to a costume shop in Salem—"Witch Capital of the World"—on Boston's North Shore. We found a race-car-driver costume for Cabot and a ladybug for Beatrice. We also found the very same Cinderella dress we'd bought for Charlotte the previous spring at Disney World. I have a photograph of her in it that breaks my heart, because that was the happiest I'd ever seen her. In Salem, though, they had the dress only in extra-large, which I took as another sign from my daughter, inflected by her wicked sense of humor. I bought it and stuffed pillows all around and I became a big fat Cinderella. I think it was the only time we laughed that whole year.

Michael's costume was a knight in shining armor, but sadly, as the weeks rolled by, that choice was becoming less and less appropriate, at least in my eyes. My husband had always been my hero, and in the past when he held my hand or reached for me it made my whole world right. But each night that autumn as he and I held each other in bed, not even his strong arms could make me feel safe. I thought, "If I can't feel protected when he holds me, I'll get closer—I'll crawl inside him if that's what it takes." So each night I took off all my clothes and asked him to do the same. I molded my naked body to his and wrapped my legs around him and pressed closer and closer, remembering the flowers we used to preserve between the pages of heavy books. If you didn't squeeze them firmly enough and left air spaces, the petals would brown and wilt. I was trying to preserve our connection this same way, trying to eliminate the gaps, but I felt that if I pushed too hard against his body I'd simply come out the other side. There was nothing solid anymore. It was as if my husband had dematerialized.

I was equally fragile, only more circumspect about it. As soon as Michael went off to work each day and the kids went off to school, I'd go up to Charlotte's room, crawl into her bed, and weep. But whenever he and the kids were home, I soldiered on, working hard to appear more functional than I was, the perfect wife and mother, losing myself in Martha Stewart hyperactivity.

One day I turned my attention to Charlotte's bathroom, where everything was still eerily, unpleasantly perfect. I stepped in and surveyed the whale-motif shower curtain and the matching whale-motif step stool. I had decorated this little room to suggest a coastal feeling of summer sun and fun, but she'd barely spent any time there. A few things were in the medicine cabinet, some towels underneath the sink. Now I decided I would set up the linen closets properly, but first I wanted to put down shelf paper, and before I could do that I needed to wipe down the shelves one last time.

During the spring, every surface had been cleared out, cleaned, sanded, and painted. I pulled over the step stool and reached up with the sponge. There on the top shelf, way in the back, was a cheap plastic angel, brushed velvet over a plastic form, covered with sparkles, wearing little faux velvet wings. Immediately I burst into tears. I picked up this little trinket and looked into the tiny face. The shelf had been freshly painted; nothing else had been left behind. The only conclusion I could draw was that this was a gift for me from Charlotte.

I put the angel in my pocket, thinking I would maybe look at it again a time or two during the day. As it turned out, it was to become my constant companion over the next several years of grieving.

Even though my "strength" was far more appearance than reality, I think my husband resented the way I seemed to be holding it together. And even as much as I understood and shared his misery, I was beginning to think he talked about Charlotte way too much. Each of us in our own way, then, was sending out the message that the other wasn't grieving "right."

Michael was, however, holding things together brilliantly at work. We had come to Boston so that he could set up a new office for a London-based venture capital firm, and all the other senior partners were Brits or South Africans. They tried to be supportive, but this was very much a stiff upper lip/carry on sort of crowd. They would call me from time to time on fishing expeditions. "How's he bearing up?" they'd ask. I'd lie and say he was doing fine.

One night Michael had dinner with a junior partner. "My daughter died last year," the younger man volunteered. "She was hit by a car." My husband was dumbfounded. Nobody at the firm knew this. This young man was offering sympathy and solidarity—"You can

talk to me"—but even as he did so he was asking Michael not to tell
the others.

It was at about this time that I began to get phone calls from
the hospital. One or two were about bills for services not covered
by insurance, but there were also the calls from the marketing
department. "Was your experience at Newton-Wellesley satisfac-
tory? Did we exceed your expectations?"

"You're kidding, right? My daughter died that day." I read them
the riot act.

I also heard from Charlotte's pediatrician in Palo Alto, the one
who had seen her after the North Carolina incident and who had
been so reluctant to enter the suspicion of malignant hyperthermia into Charlotte's record. It was a very stilted conversation. She
called to offer her condolences, but clearly there was something
else bothering her, something she couldn't quite say. It was as if
the stumbling for words and the awkward silences were an act of
contrition. I think she knew she had not been as supportive as she
might have been and now she wanted to apologize, but couldn't.
And of course her vague intimations of guilt sent me into my own
paroxysms of self-doubt, wondering if I had done all I could to get
Charlotte the care she needed.

I went back over everything Annie had told me again and again.
We had monitored Charlotte's physical activities. We had managed
her fevers with Tylenol and ibuprofen. The only reason we had not
given her the test for malignant hyperthermia was because a positive result would have made no difference. As Anne had made
clear, MH could only be managed—never cured—and, as she had
advised, we had simply assumed the worst and acted accordingly,
taking every precaution. Even when we were sure we were doing
everything we could to address that threat, we pursued every

other health concern that had ever been raised. She had been born with a small trachea, and she'd suffered from barking coughs as a baby. She also had a Bell's palsy that accounted for her crooked little grin. We looked into all of it. Then at school, on a test for muscular coordination, Charlotte did not do well. And her body had begun to change in ways that concerned me. Her legs were taking on the muscular look of a serious gymnast's, but she was just a normal little girl. I became concerned that she might have a more serious neuromuscular disorder, so we took her to Stanford Medical Center for a brain stem MRI, but the test showed nothing out of the ordinary. The most precise diagnosis that conventional medicine could come up with was "congenital anomalies." I continued to worry about multiple sclerosis, perhaps, or muscular dystrophy. What I did not want to contemplate was any association between these changes and the condition that had nearly killed her in North Carolina, and that might kill her yet.

Just before we left California, I took Charlotte to a chiropractor who used a technique called applied kinesiology. This woman was a little beyond my comfort zone, but I figured we should cover all the bases. She gave Charlotte a full physical, examined her musculature, tested her for range of motion. "Her spine is uneven," she told me, and she ordered X-rays. Then, as she was wrapping up our session, she looked at me and sighed. "This is a little girl with a lot of stuff going on."

We moved east shortly thereafter, so there was no real chance to follow up, and after Charlotte's death this woman's offhand remark haunted me. Charlotte had always been the child with more fevers, more allergies. So I called the clinic back in California and told the chiropractor what had happened and asked her about her comment. Was there something I'd missed? Had I not listened properly? What had she meant, exactly, by "a lot of stuff going on?"

There was a long pause. Then she asked me, "Did you have her adjusted?"

"No," I said. She was talking about the kind of spinal manipulation that chiropractors do.

There was another long pause. Then she said, "You should have. I should have been there. I could have saved her."

She then went on a rant about how "everybody knows" that a spinal adjustment can bring down fevers. She dressed me down for not pursuing this readily available and perfectly obvious remedy, seemingly oblivious to the fact that I was dissolving in tears at the other end of the line. I have no idea why I stayed on the phone, listening, saying nothing as I shook with rage, unless I was just taking one more opportunity to punish myself for letting my child die.

It was not long after these bruising interactions that the results came back from Charlotte's autopsy. According to the report, the findings were consistent with "the supposition of malignant hyperthermia." This lent weight to Annie's assessment, but it was still not an ironclad diagnosis. The disease leaves no trace in the tissues, so the only definitive markers are deeper down, in the genes. Anne had arranged for some of Charlotte's genetic material to be sent to the only two labs in the world equipped to conduct the more stringent genetic tests, and now those researchers wanted Michael and me, Cabot and Beatrice to provide blood as well so that the whole family's DNA could be tested. We just couldn't face that yet. How would we react to whatever we learned? Would there be more recriminations? We were fragile enough—our marriage was fragile enough—without adding the prospect of blame for things we couldn't control.

Through all these weeks of self-torture my main support was Sarah, who had returned to her life in California but was always available to me. I didn't want to abuse our relationship, especially given that counseling was her profession, but she was a dear friend who just happened to be a therapist and who had also shared the same life-altering experience that was making my life hell. We were both soldiers fighting the same war and looking for answers. The combination made it hard to resist dialing her number, which I did almost every day.

Sarah recommended a book to me, Huston Smith's *The World's Religions*, and she and I would talk for hours about our own personal theologies. She was three years ahead of me in the grieving process, but I was right there with her when she told me about her ideas of "soul groups," the notion that we pass through eternity in a cluster of souls, each one taking a different form and setting up different relationships with the others during each incarnation. She was so responsive and welcoming that it made me realize how little I had done for her when her son Wyatt had died. She had spent the last year of his life taking care of him twenty-four/ seven. He and Beatrice had been the same age, and I knew how hard it was for Sarah to see her, so we didn't do kid things together. Still, I called often and we got together to talk, but I could have done so much more. "In six months she'll be fine," I'd thought at the time. Little did I know how naive I was being. After six months, I was just getting started.

In November we joined a therapy group for families who'd lost children. This was at Parmenter Health Care in Needham, and they did a great job, especially for the kids. There were Saturday classes for children, with age-specific activities such as dance and art to help pull them out of their grief. In one project the children each made a small box in which they could put prayers and notes and keepsakes from their lost loved one. It was a bit like the "fairy holes" we'd set up for the kids on Nashawena.

While the children were involved in these sessions, the parents would have their own group therapy in the other room. These large co-ed sessions had a positive dynamic, and I found it relatively easy to be emotional, to reach and connect even when discussion was about very painful things.

But there were also separate sessions on Tuesday for fathers and on Wednesdays for mothers, and for me these turned out to be excruciating. Maybe the soul-baring talk was just too intimate for my level of repression, but it also seemed that many of the women were trapped in their grief. That included me, of course, but the distinction I'm making is that I at least wanted to find a way out. A few of them seemed content to make grief a full-time job, letting it expand to fill all the space of the missing person. I wanted to build an arsenal of weapons to fight my way back out of that dark space. I was determined to shrink the space my grief occupied and to own it, but I did not want it to grow or fester inside of me like a disease.

One woman in particular was really struggling, and really vocal, and she crowded out the rest of us so much that we had to reach out to the therapist separately to try to reach some kind of accommodation. All along, of course, I was wondering if the problem was really my own state of denial. If I were healthier, I thought, perhaps I, too, could be that dramatic and open and expansive in expressing my sorrow. I envied them their access to their sorrow. As it was, I forced myself to endure these frustrating, often depressing sessions for three years—another instance, perhaps, of guilt-ridden self-flagellation. Leaving most sessions, I would feel empty, alone, and incapable of human emotion.

Also in November a new mentor came into my life, a woman in the Boston area named Stephanie Warburg. Ten years earlier, her son had died from leukemia, and she'd started a support group for grieving parents at the Dana-Farber Cancer Institute. Mutual friends suggested that we get together, and we began to meet for lunch or have coffee. We would talk for hours, really sharing our deepest feelings about this strange and horrible thing that had happened in our lives. She said we were like combat veterans who needed to talk with other combat veterans, because nobody else could understand. Stephanie became my East Coast Sarah.

Max, Stephanie's son, had been eleven when he got sick, but his disease, chronic myelogenous leukemia, is an adult form, and it required grueling bone marrow transplants. Max had endured the search for a donor, then radiation that was almost as debilitating as the disease, followed by the insertion of the new marrow. And then he died.

There had been eighteen different people in her support group, "which meant that there were eighteen different approaches to getting through the day," she said. She told me about a nurse who also lost a son but who maintained a rock-solid faith in a Catholic version of the afterlife. There were others, she said, who had consulted with shamans. The common thread through this wide variation was a refusal to accept that death was simply the end.

"For myself," she told me, "I had to believe I'd see him again."

That was where she left it, but I had the feeling that she wanted to say more. It seemed as if she were holding back, maybe waiting until I was further along in the process. But even in her reticence she extended a promise that gave me hope. She had run her group for two years, and then, as she explained, she didn't really need it anymore. Something had given her a sense of closure. Something had put her mind to rest.

I thought about the friend of a friend who'd had the glimpse of the afterlife and found it so appealing that he didn't want to come back. I thought about Robert Swain and the "peace" and "freedom" he'd felt as death closed in on him.

What did it mean that this kind of brush with the spirit world was so common? People always described death as a movement "toward the light," or with some other, equally appealing image. Was it all just folk legend meant to comfort the survivors, or was there really something to it? Maybe dying simply releases some kind of brain chemical that gives everyone the same blissful sensations? Could something biochemical account for the fact that both Sarah and I—and now Stephanie, too—found the idea of "soul groups" and reincarnation persuasive and compelling?

Emerson didn't have much to say about the afterlife. I think somehow, for him, the "after" and the "life" seemed to be one. So I began reading Huston Smith's book and everything else I could find on death and dying, and on all the spiritual traditions from ancient times to New Age. I read Elisabeth Kübler-Ross's first book, *On Death and Dying*, the one that inspired the hospice movement and established the five stages of grief: denial, anger, bargaining, depression, and acceptance. But I also read the book she wrote after she'd moved on to the study of near-death experiences.

Late in her career, Kübler-Ross began to examine cases of people from all over the world who had been declared clinically dead, then returned to life. Based on their accounts—and supposedly she had looked into twenty thousand of these—she had become convinced that the soul leaving the body was not the end, but merely a transition to another phase of existence, one that offered a much broader perspective. She expressed this very matter-of-factly, as a respected mainstream scientist. But then, of course, her more conventionally minded colleagues heard this and decided that maybe she was not one of them after all.

Kübler-Ross had talked to patients who had come back to life in hospital rooms and were then able to describe exactly what everyone had said and done during the time they were considered "dead." In her reports, blind people who had near-death experiences sometimes came back able to describe in detail the clothing worn by those who'd been standing over their supposedly lifeless bodies. Accident victims who had "died" on impact could, after they'd been revived, relate all the details of how they were extracted from the wreckage of a crashed car. Some near-death survivors could even recall the exact license plate number of the vehicle that had run them over.

A lot of professionals who had respected Kübler-Ross's early work thought she had gone around the bend with this stuff, but her response was to say that science simply needs to remain humble in the face of mysteries we have yet to unravel. She made the spirit world sound like one of those high-pitched whistles that dogs can hear and humans can't. Just because you don't have the right instrument to pick up the sound doesn't mean the sound isn't there. Since that time there have been numerous books published by credible scientists and others that give more weight to Kübler-Ross's theories about near-death experiences. One book in particular, *Proof of Heaven*, detailed the experience of a neurosurgeon as he lay in a lifeless coma for a week. It laid out in full scientific detail how this near-death experience could not be explained by any brain functioning.

I loved Kübler-Ross and Eben Alexander's descriptions of the afterlife, but particularly the fact that they weren't just repeating assumptions based on some religious traditions. They were making a case based on alleged firsthand experiences, supposedly observed with clinical detachment. But what resonated the most for me was the way they both described the people waiting for us on the other side. They said we were met by the people who had loved us most. It was like the image of the boat being received on the other shore from the poem at Charlotte's funeral. Her soul group. Awaiting her arrival.

In November we went to Naushon to return to the Aisle of Beeches, where we'd installed a plaque in Charlotte's memory on the large stone that I'd hugged, crying. On that trip I took some of my new spiritual library with me. I had been calmed and comforted by what I'd been reading, but when I stood in among the memorials in that dappled sunlight and confronted the reality of Charlotte's name and dates, I came unglued all the same. I stayed there crouched and leaning into the stone, weeping once again until I fell asleep.

If death is so blissful for the dying, I kept asking myself, why does it have to be so devastating for those of us left behind? I thought again about the Pietà, and all the mothers through all of human history bringing flowers to the graves of their children. Was grief, agony, and loss all we could expect in this world? That's where the consolation of religion is supposed to come in. But what if that consolation isn't enough? Where do we draw the line between reasonable faith and nutty magical thinking? That's when it occurred to me that on Naushon we never drew the line. On Naushon the boundary between the natural and the supernatural had always been negotiable. The spirit world was never discussed—we were WASPs, after all—but it was always assumed.

Maybe for the first time I began to think seriously about all the island's ghost stories. I thought about Kübler-Ross's image of the dog whistle and the way that science had pushed belief in spirits to the margins. Or had the hubbub of technology simply diminished our ability to perceive, the way television and the Internet supposedly diminish our attention spans? Had the "unnatural" world of hustle and bustle and concrete, steel, and climate control in our homes simply drowned out a natural ability to perceive the world of spirit? Have we literally insulated ourselves from it? By spending more time listening, could we regain that ability? With enough focus, could we begin to reconnect? Was that the "religion teaching" bequeathed by my family that would actually do me some good?

The ghost is a standard feature of most old New England houses, where floors creak and windows rattle and doors bang in the breeze even without the help of spirits. Sometimes the stories seem to be passed along as part of a playful mythology, like Santa Claus or the tooth fairy. But on Naushon, and within my family generally, the stories were much more matter-of-fact. Not that everyone, if forced to articulate their belief system, would have insisted that the ghosts were real. I'm sure there were skeptics, but the question simply never came up. No one was ever asked to take a position. So to us, as kids, having ghosts seemed about as remarkable as having a refrigerator.

My great-great-uncle Don, the one who died of a ruptured appendix in Stone House, has been encountered dozens of times in the halls, sometimes running with a football. Emerson's daughter, my great-great-grandmother Edith, often appears at dinner, as does John Murray Forbes's daughter Sarah.

Julia, the wife of a cousin, had once been a frequent visitor to the island, and she'd become pals with another, older cousin named Lawrie. She'd been away for a while, and on her first summer back, she came up to the house describing how she'd just run into Lawrie at the first bridge and had a lovely chat with him. What she didn't know was that Lawrie had died the previous year.

Several years earlier, Julia had calmly inquired of her dinner guests if they could see the old ship captain pacing back and forth in front of the fireplace while they were dining. Ever the gracious hostess, she had sat and quietly watched him for twenty minutes before even mentioning it.

On the island we have a jack-of-all-trades, Laurence Sevigny, a New Hampshireman who comes down every spring, stays at Mansion House, and does whatever repairs need to be done. A couple of years ago, I ran into him and he seemed slightly shaken. I asked him why.

"I had two pretty darn weird experiences this week," he said.

"What do you mean?"

"I have been alone all week and no one is on the island with kids, but one night this week I heard children running and laughing in the halls while I was trying to sleep. A bit later somebody climbed into bed with me in the middle of the night. They didn't push me or anything. Nothing mean. But it really flipped me out."

I could relate. On Naushon once, when Charlotte was very small, I went downstairs to get a bottle for her in the night and I had an eerie sense that someone was following me. It was real enough for the hair on the back of my neck to stand up. I felt as if someone were in my space, but I couldn't see or hear anything. I wanted to move away, but I couldn't, because this presence stayed with me.

"The next day," Laurence went on, "I was in the basement and I heard footsteps on the first floor. I called, 'Hello!' and I heard somebody call back, 'Hello,' so I called again and heard the 'Hello' response again, and then again, along with footsteps. The steps and the sound of the voice were moving toward the kitchen, so I went right up. But nobody was there. And Moose [his dog] was right there with me, and she started to bark and act real strange. Her eyes were going back and forth like she was watching something that I couldn't see."

The next spring when I saw Laurence again, I asked him where Moose was.

"I can't bring her anymore," he said. "She gets too bothered by the ghosts."

The tales of the supernatural were not limited to people. In the mid-1800s John Murray Forbes had a much beloved pony on the island for the younger children to ride. For thirty-one years she was on Naushon, and one day she vanished. She was last seen grazing quietly by a gate near the farm. She disappeared with a family terrier as well, but the terrier returned home ten days later none the worse for wear. Her mysterious disappearance has never been explained. John Murray Forbes wrote at the time that she "disappeared into the Elysian fields where all good ponies go."

When we moved into Mansion House, I was actually afraid to sleep there alone because of the ghost of Mr. Bowdoin. Meanwhile, we were pouring a fortune into restoring the place, so my discomfort was pretty inconvenient. One night I stood by myself upstairs in the hall in the main part of the 1809 structure and I said out loud, "Excuse me, Mr. Bowdoin, I'm scared of you and I don't want to see you. I know you're here, and I'm not saying you have to leave. But we love this house just as you do and I really don't want you to scare us. You can stay, but please leave us alone. And whatever you do, please do not scare the children!"

I have felt a comfortable kinship with Mr. Bowdoin ever since. I still greet him by name every time I arrive, and say good-bye to him every time I leave.

The Forbes association with ghosts extended to the mainland as well. One summer we hired a house sitter for our place in Milton while we were on Naushon. Her name was Lizzy, and when we returned to Milton she told my father that she kept passing some kind of presence on the stairs. She went on to describe being in the kitchen, and then for some reason felt compelled to go into the living room. She went and stood in the doorway, where she saw an older man with white hair and a white beard, sitting serenely with a Forbes tartan across his lap but with an expression on his face that said, "This is my space; don't come in."

"Uncle Alex," my father told her. "Don's brother. The one who built this house."

All this may sound nutty, but it inspired me because I so desperately needed something more than a door slamming shut. Game over. The end. I needed a new perspective that would unite my ordinary experience with the new state of being that Charlotte had entered. I needed a single container that could include both the natural and the supernatural, and yet was more substantive than Emerson's gauzy romanticism.

I didn't know it, but that's what Stephanie had been waiting to offer me, as soon as I was ready.

We spent our first Thanksgiving without Charlotte with Anne and Harry at their home in Maryland. I sent out a card that was a photograph of our family—all five of us—standing on Baker Beach in San Francisco, waving good-bye to the Golden Gate Bridge. On the inside I wrote, "We are thankful for the support of family and friends during difficult times and we are thankful that we moved to Boston . . ." It was very important for me to try to set the tone for people in how to respond to us. I wanted it to show some strength, some self-reliance.

When December came I was forced to tamp down the pain even more and deal with the usual hubbub of Christmas shopping and children's holiday events. The only holiday decor that brought me any festive cheer was the lights. The elves aroused in me an irritation so great I wanted to kick them. It was an odd, dark, macabre expression of my Kübler-Ross anger phase. Perhaps not so curiously, the ladies in my grief group all felt the same way and shared several laughs about the thought of the bereaved crazy ladies kicking elves and shouting, "Merry F-ing Christmas!"

Feeling the need for more life around us, my family and I also decided to get a dog, which would be delivered after the first of the year. In California we'd had a beloved Jack Russell terrier named Waldo who'd been hit by a car the year before, when we were in Boston looking at real estate. Michael wept when we got the news about the accident. I didn't. When we told the children, they sat there in silence for about five seconds, and then Charlotte cocked her head to the side and said, "Um, can we get a hamster?"

Snow came early that year, and by the middle of the month the

Boston area was covered by a blanket of white. I thought of *Dubliners*, and how Joyce had described the snow "falling faintly through the universe . . . upon all the living and the dead." I had always loved snow, and this year I found the silent insulation especially comforting.

But December 23 was Charlotte's birthday, not an easy day for stoicism. She would have been seven.

We went to visit my mother in Concord and the drive past great-great-great-grandfather Emerson's shuttered home in Concord made the day seem dreary. We spent the afternoon sharing stories, trying to keep the conversation light. It reminded me of the Saturdays after chores when Mum would have formal tea with cheap grape jelly and cream cheese on Ritz or saltine crackers. But the tea itself was always an exotic (and very expensive) variety of Lapsang souchong named after Houqua (Hu Kwa), John Murray Forbes's benefactor in the China trade. It has a smoky flavor from being dried over pine fires. This one gourmet indulgence would be followed by a dinner of baked beans and hot dogs, iceberg lettuce with Ken's Italian dressing (one of the four meals in Mum's repertoire).

My mother and I also slipped away to buy stocking stuffers at the Concord Five and Dime, another family tradition steeped in Yankee frugality. During my childhood, Santa didn't bring big presents; he just filled stockings. And according to the tags we'd sometimes find on our shiny new pencils and toothbrushes, he often shopped at Osco's Drug and the five-and-dime.

Walking along the streets of Emerson and Thoreau's old town, I asked my mother to tell me what she thought about God and the afterlife, and her views seemed much more like mine than I'd ever realized. She, too, said she felt much closer to God in nature—even in gardening—than in any church, but that she appreciated ritual and, like me, found meaning and comfort in communion, and in singing and reciting scriptural passages in unison. Then she reminded me of how, in the early seventies, she and my father, along with several other families, branched off from the Unitarian Church in Milton and began to gather in a small chapel that had been donated to the parish by my mother's grandmother. For a while, they "rolled their own" small religious service, which was focused on ethical behavior but was as likely to draw from Aesop's fables as the Bible.

My mother and I had never been close when I was a girl, but we had become good friends as I progressed into adulthood, and this image of her own period of searching helped to draw us even closer. In the seventies, after she and my father divorced, she'd continued her efforts at reinventing herself emotionally and spiritually, first by switching to the Episcopalian Church and then by attending "personal growth" workshops. But the God of her imagination was such a male force, she told me, that she never took to the "Goddess movement" that was so in vogue, despite dabbling in it for a while during that decade.

But my mother had come a long way spiritually, and I was learning from her daily. Before we left her house that bleak December day she said, "You may take this as an insult, but I think this process is going to make you better people. You are going to come through this process more humble." I asked her what she meant. "Well, you've been handed an awful lot. You've got a lot of gifts. I think this is a humbling process and at the very end of it you'll be in a better place." I think she was right, but at that moment it was a difficult message to receive, and slim consolation. Frankly, I had the same urge to kick her as I did those pesky holiday elves that tormented me all around town.

When we came home that evening, Cabot and Beatrice insisted on having a cake and candles and singing "Happy Birthday" for their sister, but I simply couldn't. The tears came streaming and my throat closed up. I smiled and pretended to sing but I was just mouthing the words.

After I put the kids to bed, I had to get out of the house, so I drove down to see the big oak tree through which I'd watched the sun go down the day Charlotte had died. The neighbors had installed a huge, illuminated pink star there as a memorial to her. For a few moments I sat crying silently. Then I began banging my fists on the steering wheel screaming, "Where are you?!" It was not my finest moment.

Two days later, when Christmas came, we let the kids open the gifts in their stockings, then went directly to the airport. We had lined up a totally absurd trip to Bogotá, Colombia, where Michael's sister Jeanne lived. We needed to get away, and we needed to blot out this particularly "Kodak moment" holiday, which we managed to do by spending nine hours in an airplane. Flying for the first few times as a family after Charlotte's death, I would daydream that perhaps the plane would go down and we all would die and be reunited with Charlotte. If we were all together, I found this thought perversely comforting, but on the few occasions that I flew alone I developed great anxiety about the plane going down with me on it. How could I do that to my children and husband? We were in so much pain already. I could not die and leave them. I had to stay alive and healthy for them.

Jeanne's husband did some kind of work for the U.S. government, which meant that we had access to an armored car with bulletproof glass and a heavily armed driver to be our escort into the countryside. To add to the absurdity, our three-year-old, Beatrice, exposed to Spanish by way of our Peruvian nanny, Maria, was the one we called on when we needed an interpreter.

Leaving the city limits, we started to see tanks and other military equipment, which brought to the surface the thought that had been lingering ever since the plan originated: "Maybe we'll die down there." We hiked up to a mountaintop overlook with a panoramic view of a lush green valley with gorgeous lakes, the kids rode donkeys, and we had a picnic. The whole experience was completely surreal, and then a few days later we flew home. Afterward, my friend Sarah described the whole excursion as temporary insanity in the form of a death wish, again fueled by guilt.

Before we'd left for Bogotá we had deputized Maria to fly to D.C. to pick up our new Jack Russells. I had chosen one dog, and, typically, Michael had said, "Let's get two." So when we came back from South America we were greeted by Bandina, about six months, and Lindy Loo, who'd been born just around the time of Charlotte's death.

Jack Russells are definitely not for everyone. A cross between a beagle and a fox terrier, this breed is adorable and very smart, which is why they're used so much on TV and in the movies. But they have a mind of their own, which makes them very difficult. I love the way they tilt their heads and cock their ears as if they're really processing what you say and want to give you a thoughtful response, then toss their head and strut away. But here as in so many undertakings during this time, we overestimated the amount of energy and focus we would have available for training the animals. In fact, we had none, so these dogs remained completely out of control.

Shortly after our new pets arrived, my Saltonstall grandmother died. Everyone was afraid to tell me, but in fact I couldn't have been happier for her. She'd suffered from Alzheimer's, so the grandmother I knew had faded away ten years earlier. Up until then she'd enjoyed a healthy and enviable life, and the service at the assisted-living facility she'd shared with my grandfather was truly a celebration of that life. I felt closer to her that day than I had in years.

The Saltonstalls had always appeared more austere and dour than the Forbes clan, but they were actually much warmer beneath the surface. Many of my Saltonstall relatives were teachers and headmasters, and I think, as a group, they pretty much embodied all the virtues like "truth" and "fidelity" that you see on school crests. In the Forbes family, it was more typical for the "deep" ones to become artists or join an ashram. The rest simply went into banking.

Charlotte's middle name was Saltonstall, so I thought it was very important that she learn something about this family. She was only about three years old when I first brought her back from California to meet Grancy and Grampa Salt. They took us up to Salem, where the old family manse is located, and where the Peabody Essex Museum contains rooms full of Saltonstall furnishings and artwork. I have photographs of my austere, six-foot-four grandfather Robert Saltonstall, proudly holding the hand of my little two-foot-tall Charlotte, showing her around while showing her off.

This first winter after Charlotte's death the snow cover stuck around until March, and as a family we took a ski vacation in Utah. A good friend owns the resort at Snowbird, and every year he invites a big group of friends for a long weekend. This had become a family tradition for us while we lived in California, and I guess we wanted to present an image of getting back to normal, even if we weren't even close.

Out west that year the snowfall was the heaviest on record, and we were in a lodge at the base of the mountain that was built like a bunker to withstand avalanches. I was with people I cared about, and the layers of clothing and the goggles and helmets we all wore added to my feeling of being armored and insulated and very safe. The snow kept falling, and each morning our friend the owner would open up the mountain early so that we could have fresh tracks on the exquisite powder. The physical activity was just what I needed. I was ensconced in a group but alone when I needed to be, so it was the perfect combination of isolation and togetherness, with plenty of exertion to simply wear myself out.

On the gondola rides up the mountain I stared at the trees, wondering what it must feel like to be a limb weighed down with so much snow and ice all winter. Was it comforting? Did it start out like a sweater and gradually build to the point of unbearable heaviness? Was it a huge relief when spring came and the snow dropped off? What about when the branch just broke?

Our room back at the lodge was like a womb, with big windows looking out on the floodlit snow, which kept on falling, so much so that the lifts closed several times. But I never felt cut off or claustrophobic. I felt safe and warm, with each snowflake adding to my protective blanket. When we'd come back, Michael would take the kids to the heated outdoor pool, but I couldn't do swimming pools—Charlotte had loved them too much. I'd lie in the room and watch the people skiing down on their last runs of the day.

On the third night I lay in bed watching the snow drift down and I felt a huge sob catch in my throat. I needed to get rid of this knot, so I forced it out, and suddenly the floodgates just blew open and the tears came and once they came they would not stop. I sobbed so hard for so long that my abdominal muscles got sore. My whole body was shaking so much that I got out of bed and went to sit on the couch. Even so, there was enough commotion to wake up Michael, and he came over and sat with me. I found his presence alone comforting, but when he cradled me in his arms I came unglued. The renewed strength he found to be there for me was the final element I needed. It now felt safe for me to completely fall apart.

I cried for hours while he held me and silently rocked me back and forth. Usually I don't like to be held when I'm really troubled— I'm more like a wounded dog who simply wants to skulk off alone. But that night I relished it. I was astonished by my own vulnerability. I kept saying, "I can't stop crying." Then near dawn I asked him to do the "snug as a bug" thing we often did for our children and I recall my mother doing for me when I was small. So he wrapped me up in my blanket and carried me to bed, swaddling all the covers around me and tucking them in under my feet.

When the sun came up, my eyes were swollen shut. I had cried until I couldn't cry anymore. I had reached the bottom, so now it was time to begin working my way back up.

8

Angel Day

When I told my new friend Stephanie about how I'd finally melted down in Utah, I think she saw this as the sign she'd been waiting for. In her eyes, I was now ready to join her on what she called "our side of the fence."

Stephanie and I had been getting together for lunch for some time, and she'd been very open about her own experience of being stripped down psychologically to the bare bone. She'd been far more reticent, however, about sharing with me how she'd managed to move on from that very dark place.

Sitting in a café in Brookline, she began to open up a bit more, telling me about an experience she'd had shortly after her son's death.

"This was in '91," she said. "The summer. I was lying down, in this sort of middle state between waking and sleeping, and I felt his hand."

She stopped to look at me for a moment. It was as if she were gauging my reaction, but I wasn't judging. I was simply listening, completely there with her.

"I thought I'd squeeze back as sort of a test," she went on.

I smiled and nodded.

"His hand stayed in my hand. Then I felt a kiss on the cheek."

My own eyes welled up with tears as I thought about my own moments of sensing Charlotte's presence. Just a few months before this meeting with Stephanie I'd had a powerful dream that I had not shared with anyone. We'd been gathered on the steps in the house of my childhood, 610 Harland Street, for our annual family portrait, only this time it was my nuclear family with Michael rather than my siblings and parents. We were all posed on the landing and Charlotte was sitting next to me. I had my arm around her, and I could feel the warmth of her body next to mine and the softness of her cheek pressed into mine. In my dream I began to question if in fact I was actually dreaming or if this was a visit from Charlotte. I decided to press my cheek harder into hers to see what happened. She pushed back. I woke up immediately, beaming and utterly convinced that for that one moment I had in fact regained physical contact with my daughter.

I took Stephanie's hand, and said, "You know, I'm not really religious in a traditional sense. But there just has to be more, right? Something more than when you die you're dead."

She looked at me for a moment. Then she said, "There's a woman I think you ought to see."

"Who? Tell me."

Stephanie still seemed a bit hesitant. "I usually wait a long time before mentioning this. People think it's weird."

"Believe me," I said, "I'm ready for anything."

She took a deep breath, and then she began telling me how she'd been part of a group gathered at the Arlington Street Church in Boston to meet with a medium. The woman who invited her had lost her husband on Pan Am Flight 103, the plane that had been blown apart by a terrorist bomb over Lockerbie, Scotland, in 1988. Stephanie was one of hundreds of people in the church auditorium, and the medium came right up to her and said, "You've lost a child." Stephanie was flabbergasted, especially when the medium began to offer familiar descriptions of her son Max, as well as fragmented impressions of how he'd died. "He's doing well," the medium told Stephanie. "He loves you."

Understandably, my friend became hooked on the possibility of being able to communicate with the dead. Shortly afterward she was in London, where a cousin of hers directed her to the College of Psychics. This led to an encounter with a fairly inept psychic-in-training who had her lie down surrounded by candles. She said it was all very depressing and not helpful. Then, back in the States, she followed one lead after another and had various encounters with what she described as a variety of charlatans and cranks. Eventually she discovered the woman she now wanted me to meet.

"She's the real deal," Stephanie told me.

Their first encounter had been over the phone, and when Stephanie arranged the conversation she'd made sure that the medium knew nothing about her, and certainly nothing about the fact that her son had died. Stephanie used a fake name, and when she got on the line she let the medium have the first word. "Are you the person who lost a child?" the woman began. It was a good place to start.

"I see your son," she went on. "He liked woodworking. He's holding up a wooden sign with a wavy bottom."

"That's when the tears came," Stephanie told me. She knew the sign immediately. Max had made it in woodshop at school. It said, "Shhh! Sleeping."

"I know what you're talking about," Stephanie had said. "But the bottom's straight."

"No," the medium had insisted. "You check it out."

She was right.

Stephanie was still running her support group back then, and she was so excited about her new discovery that she wanted to invite the medium to talk to the group at Dana-Farber, but the hospital said no. Instead, the social workers who supervised the group arranged for them to meet at a nearby Unitarian church.

"Hundreds of people showed up," Stephanie said. "She made all these eerily accurate connections. She was utterly convincing."

But I didn't need to be convinced; I was ready to open up to a different set of perceptions and ideas. I'd begun haunting bookstores, and reading even more widely. What I appreciated most were the matter-of-fact accounts that dispensed with gauzy theory, or any hard sell, and simply gave reasonable, sane-sounding reports of experiences beyond the conventional. The words of one psychic, Suzane Northrop, resonated most: "If you come to believe that death is not the end, you will release a limited potential in yourself. You will also have conquered your greatest fear." This is exactly what I found I wanted to do.

I was amazed by my own eagerness to meet Stephanie's medium, but equally surprised that when I told Michael what I was up to, he didn't respond as if I'd gone nuts. Michael is a very data-driven kind of man, wedded to spreadsheets and the facts and figures therein. It wasn't as if I didn't have my own doubts, of course.

When I bought the ticket to hear her speak I paid in cash rather than with a credit card. If this woman was a fake, I didn't want to make it too easy for her to come up with "messages" by providing any more information than I needed.

Was I worried about what my friends or family would think? There was enough eccentric behavior in Forbes family history that the only thing my loopy aristocratic clan could object to in my meeting was the setting: a big auditorium at a Holiday Inn in Worcester, Massachusetts.

About an hour west of Boston, Worcester is a city with little to recommend it but the Jesuit College of the Holy Cross, alma mater of Clarence Thomas, and Clark University, the venue, oddly enough, for the only lecture Sigmund Freud ever gave in the United States.

There were about five hundred people in the audience when the medium—I'll call her Margaret—came onstage. My first thought was how very untheatrical the whole scene was. I guess my only exposure to spiritualism was from watching old movies where overdressed ladies sat at tables in Victorian drawing rooms and heard lots of tapping. But there were no candles here, no celestial-sounding music, just this rather small woman stepping out and beginning to talk—fast—with a strong New York accent. In those first moments this encounter seemed about as spiritual as a real estate seminar.

But then I began to wonder if there was something wrong with my eyes, or maybe I had a migraine coming on. I blinked, but I kept seeing a wavy outline around her body that moved with her as she moved back and forth across the speaking platform, and which then began to undulate like a lava lamp. Stage lighting? I looked around and all the way up to the ceiling, and the only illumination was of the hideous, bright-as-day conference room type. Eventually I said to myself, "Okay. She's surrounded by an aura. That's what's happening. This is an aura. Either that, or I really am losing it."

She began by laying out the ground rules for the session. She then led us into a guided meditation, asking everyone to imagine taking an elevator up and up, then stepping out into an open field. I closed my eyes and tried to concentrate. After a bit I saw myself in a setting like the opening shot from *The Sound of Music*—Julie Andrews surrounded by jagged mountains, a beautiful meadow, and red and yellow flowers. I was just settling into the sensations, seeing the colors, smelling the fresh grassy smells, when in the distance I saw Charlotte. All of a sudden she was in my face wagging her head side to side as she often did—my little girl saying, "Hi, Mummy! Hi, Mummy!"

I didn't shriek with joy. I wasn't overcome. I simply smiled.

"I've heard of this," I said to myself. "Wow. I can access it. This is great."

And that's when the first wave of overwhelming relief washed over me. My little girl running up to me was happy, grinning ear to ear. She was safe. She was healthy. Wherever she was, and however much she'd left behind, she looked like she was having a grand old time.

"Now I'll take messages," Margaret said. "I never know what's going to come through, but if it sounds like I'm talking about somebody you know, put your hand up. I'll just keep talking. It usually becomes obvious who I'm talking about."

She began to wander through the audience, keeping up her rapid-fire patter. "It's someone over here . . . ," she'd say, and then she'd amble in that direction. "It's a man. Fifty-six years old and he had a heart condition."

"Pretty broad brush, Margaret," the skeptic in me kept saying. "No points for that one."

But then she'd drill down. "He has three daughters . . . There's a real issue with the son." Three hands went up, all seated next to one another.

Then she came through with the zinger. "Why am I seeing a remote control? It looks to me like a remote control in his casket."

"Omigod!" one of the girls said. "We buried Daddy with the remote!"

Pretty cute. But how could I know these three girls hadn't been planted in the audience? The shill in the audience—Carnival Huckster 101.

"Okay, I'm getting something—I'm getting a young child." She began to look in my direction. "I'm getting a girl. She's about seven years old. She died very suddenly. She has other siblings. I'm getting a hot fever."

I put my hand up and she came over.

She began talking about the two other children, a boy and a girl. Skeptical or not, I began to shake. Then she said the thing that changed my entire view of life, the universe, everything.

"She wants to acknowledge something you carry in your pocket all the time. It's sort of white and sparkly."

I burst into tears. I was so overcome that the woman seated next to me reached over to make sure I didn't fall out of my chair.

Then I reached into my pocket and pulled out the angel I'd found on the shelf in the linen closet in Charlotte's room.

"She said she put it on a shelf for you to find," Margaret said.

I had known that in my heart. Now it was confirmed. This one detail also confirmed—at least to any level of proof I might require—that this woman really was in touch with Charlotte.

I was still crying, still trembling, as Margaret went on. "She also wants to acknowledge something your neighbors did to honor her. It's bright pink. I see electricity . . . in a tree."

She began to describe the split-rail fence along Orchard Avenue, the rolling field, and the big oak tree where our neighbors had put the big star with pink lights just before Christmas. I had no way to account for this. It made no sense according to any of the rules of the universe as I understood them. And yet it simply was.

This complete stranger then went on to talk about Michael, and about the kids, and even about certain specifics of Charlotte's death. As the tears streamed down my face, the logical, Episcopalian part of me kept struggling, still resisting the idea and wondering if I was being hoodwinked. Later, I rehearsed the arguments for and against: I'd learned of this session only twelve hours before it took place, paid cash, and never given my name or any identifying information. When Charlotte died, there had been nothing in the papers, not even an obituary. If Margaret had known my real name, if she'd had a team of investigators with computers and several days to prepare, she might have dug up some of this information. But as for the angel—I'd never even told Michael about it. I hadn't told the kids. No one on the planet knew about that angel I carried in my pocket but me . . . and Charlotte.

I walked out of the auditorium weak-kneed and trembling, but also on a cushion of air. I was thinking, "Okay, my daughter has come through and she's okay. She's more than okay. She's been dead for seven months, and I think I just had a conversation with her!"

I made a beeline for a woman seated at a registration table in the foyer. When she looked up I said, "I would like to book a private session."

I made the appointment, but this time it would have to include Michael as well. He had to experience this. But even in my excitement, my old-school skepticism had not entirely dissipated. I booked this second session using the credit card one of my employees uses and that carries her name, not mine.

There was a reception for the attendees, but I had to get out of the Holiday Inn and decompress. I went out to the parking lot and for the next two hours simply sat in my car. In part, I sat there because I was shaking so much I wasn't sure I could drive. For a while there I thought I might have to get a room. But more than my temporary inability to operate heavy machinery, I simply wanted to savor every second of this experience. This was the first real joy I'd felt in half a year, and Charlotte had been at the very center of it. She'd shared it with me!

After I'd calmed down a bit, I called Michael to tell him about Margaret and what she'd said and what I'd experienced, and I was so surprised by how receptive he was that I broke down crying all over again. Whatever private misgivings he might have had about consulting a medium, he could hear that I'd gone from despair to elation in just a few hours. No fool, he—he wanted some of that for himself. He was very much on board with the idea of the private session I'd just booked for the two of us in June.

I was so desperate to keep this connection alive that for the next several nights I couldn't sleep. It wasn't just that Charlotte had appeared to me and given me messages. It was that she seemed so very, very happy. It no longer seemed as if she'd been erased or had dropped into the abyss. It felt as if all three of my children could be part of my life again. Cabot and Beatrice still need lots of attention, but my Charlotte—she's fine. I had to make sure she was in good hands, as if I'd left her with a sitter. She'd gone away, but now the absence was more like having a son or daughter who's gone off to camp or to college. And because I'd seen her thriving in her new space, a lot of my anxiety dissipated. I could picture her now, running through vast fields filled with fragrant flowers. She was so joyous that she would leap and jump. The setting in my imagination was not unlike the wide-open fields and gently sloping hills of Naushon, only with more color, and a crystal clear blue sky, and always plenty of sunshine and warmth.

I no longer had to deal with her missing out on life, or the tragedy of her dying young, but simply my missing her. It even crossed my mind that it was selfish of me to want to cling to her when obviously she was now in such a good place.

After that one life-changing moment with Margaret, I felt hope for the first time in almost a year. In the weeks and months to come, I couldn't always hold to that, but it set a new tone for a healthier way of grieving—and, indeed, of living. I moved in and out of that healthier register, but when I was there I got a glimmer of how it might be possible to reconnect with life, and that life could be worth living again, despite our loss. Charlotte was living life. Some kind of different life, but it was good and she was happy and well cared for. That knowledge allowed me to renew my commitment to living my life as well.

A few weeks later, of course, the misery and the pain were back in full swing. My arms ached at the elbows where I'd held Charlotte as a baby, and my breasts felt full the way they used to while nursing. Full, ready to let down and feed the baby. But there was no baby. I had weaned my last child over a year prior to Charlotte's death.

"Let's have another baby," I told Michael. A cousin of mine had lost a child to SIDS and then went on to have another. I admired the way he and his wife had seemingly bore their grief yet managed to keep their family healthy, intact, and growing.

Michael said, "Okay."

I still needed to be surrounded by new life—any life, for that matter. Part of that desire was acted out with the silly dogs, our new Jack Russells. The breeder had gotten things off to a bad start by dressing up Lindy like a baby. When the dogs came to us,

Beatrice began to dress her up in doll clothing. I couldn't help myself and bought both dogs yellow rain slickers and navy blue woolen peacoats with red collars and brass buttons. I alternated between being embarrassed and entertained by the whole spectacle. My relatives, of course, couldn't bear to think about anything so *Legally Blonde* as dressing up cute little dogs in funny clothes.

We took the animals to Naushon with us, and that spring on opening weekend we had a young couple as guests, along with their three-year-old daughter, Lizzie. On Saturday morning some of my cousins rode behind the house on horseback and Lindy Loo ran straight across their path, causing the horse to rear up and kick her in the head in the process. My brother came running up to the house saying, "Lindy Loo's dead," and somehow Karen heard it as "Lizzie's dead" and let out a loud and bloodcurdling wail. That instant of terror took me back to that first moment when I had to accept that my own child was gone, and I began to cry as well. We quickly sorted it all out, and by the time we got out to the road Lindy was conscious. We took her down to the stable, where the stable manager bandaged her up, and she was fine.

When we showed up in June for our session with Margaret, once again at the very unmystical Holiday Inn, we introduced ourselves simply as Michael and Sukey.

"Sukey's not your given name," Margaret said. I nodded politely at what was hardly a rock 'em, sock 'em insight from beyond the grave. Not too many "Sukeys" appear on official birth certificates.

"Well, it's very important to this person coming through that you acknowledge your formal name," she said.

Michael and I looked at each other. We had come to hear from

Charlotte, but then I remembered what Margaret had said about having no control over who spoke to her or what they wanted to convey.

After a moment I realized she was talking about my grandfather, David Cabot Forbes. He always called me Suzannah—never Sukey. He'd always been very concerned about certain proprieties. Then again, he was also the one who loved to sail nude, the ringleader for Naushon's multigenerational skinny dips on Silver Beach. We stumbled through various other voices with other bizarre, seemingly trivial concerns.

"What is this thing with horses?" she asked.

"Horses?"

"You have horses in the family? I gotta tell you somewhere in your family somebody lost horses because I've got two horses coming through."

"Oh?"

"I can't help thinking it's a grandfather on your side, Sukey."

"That makes sense. My grandfather was fond of horses."

"Yeah. I know there was one who passed who he must have been quite fond of because the horse comes through with him. Was that horse almost palomino looking?"

"I don't recall his ever having had a palomino."

"You know, he's buried behind your house."

"No way."

"You check into this." She was confident that she was correct, I had to give her that.

Later, I did, and found out that my skinny-dipping grandfather's favorite horse had been a palomino named Spider that he buried in the field just behind Mansion House.

This whole thing was just too strange. It got even more strange when she started hearing from Michael's two dead uncles, one who'd died from a brain tumor, the other who'd died in a fire. Margaret had it right about both of them.

And then she said, "There's a young child coming through." Once again I felt as if I were lifting off the ground.

We'd said nothing about having lost a child. Then again, anybody could have guessed that one. What's the most likely reason a youngish couple would go to see a medium? But then she veered off to talk about my son, Cabot. "He planted something in the garden," she said. "In honor of your daughter. It looks like a little flower. It looks like a cluster of daisies. They're plastic and they're white with a yellow center and they're planted in your garden."

Another electric charge went through my body. "Yes, that's true," I said, trying to hold steady. "But they're blue with a yellow center."

She said, "I'm getting that they're white."

"No," I said, "they're blue."

When I went home and checked I saw that they were white. I'd misremembered. Margaret—or maybe I should say Charlotte—had it right.

Then it got eerier still. Margaret went on and on about how someone had known there was something wrong with Charlotte, someone who knew that she was not going to have a long life.

"Who's Anne . . . maybe Annie?" she said. And it just kept going. She seemed to be describing Sarah and her husband, George. Then both Max and Wyatt came through, even though Sarah and Stephanie had never met, and Charlotte had never been with Max. There was some confusion when Margaret began to talk about the "Sarah" figure struggling with the loss of a child. Of course she was, but Wyatt had died long before. "No, this is newer, a more recent struggle." Later, I checked with Sarah and found out that she'd just had a miscarriage. She hadn't told me for fear of upsetting me.

I began to understand what it meant that this process of Margaret's was neither linear nor rational, but as free-form as a dream.

She then described an arched lattice with trellises and said the little girl was showing this to her. "That's where we lived," I said. Margaret looked at me and asked, "Now would that be called a ranch?" I was a WASP from Boston with an Irish Catholic husband from Maryland. We'd said nothing about having lived in California. We'd certainly never said anything about owning forty acres up in the Santa Cruz Mountains. And for sure, in Margaret's presence, we'd never referred to the place, as we always did among ourselves, as "the ranch."

Then she described the hawk, the beautiful, fierce bird that had shown up at our home in Weston the day Charlotte died. I had been intrigued when it perched on our gatepost, then flew up into a tree, where it stayed for several days watching us. Even more so when it made intense, protracted eye contact with me and Michael. On two occasions it held me in its gaze for a good ten minutes. I'd thought at the time that it might be Charlotte's spirit in some way, come back to watch over us.

After my first session with Margaret I'd been in a pleasant state of shock. Now I was euphoric.

Michael looked happier than I'd seen him in months, but I could already see him beginning to do the "spreadsheet" for this experience in his head, trying to reconcile these new revelations with his existing belief system. With Michael, everything ultimately came

down to analytics. He and a friend used to pose philosophical questions and then try to answer them with equations. But as Emerson
wrote, "Nature does not love a calculator."

We were both still mired in grief, but at least for me the nature of grieving had fundamentally changed. It was a "felt" experience, and because of that I had a fundamental attitude shift, or
at least the beginning of one. Knowing where Charlotte was and
that she was happy and well meant that I could miss her without
worrying about her, a reassurance that allowed me to focus on
coming back to life myself.

Ultimately, though, I think Michael's Catholic belief system
and his analytical way of looking at things created much more in-
terference. These messages coming in from another realm required a shift in worldview that may have been more far-reaching
than he could manage. Complicating the issue was his self-image
as a can-do, in-control person. He simply wasn't ready to surrender his entire way of looking at the world. He needed to manage
his world, not surrender to it, and a big part of that effort was
bound up with the idea of an all-knowing and all-powerful God
who was accessible to him and always on his side. But it was his
belief that this was the way the world was supposed to work that
also fueled his anger. After all, he'd done everything "right." He'd
been a good husband and father, he'd made a lot of money and
given some to charity, gone to church and said all the prayers, and
yet he'd still lost Charlotte, which left him, deep down, I believe,
like some character out of a Russian novel, wanting to rail against
God. On the other hand, his strong Catholic faith created huge
conflicts for him about what to do with all that rage.

William James said that an emotion is a physical response to a
stimulus, whether or not it enters into our awareness. (Our

awareness of the body's response is called a feeling.) I've always been sensitive to the physical nature of my emotions, and I was desperate to purge the negative ones, so I began to spend a lot of time running. I felt that I had to get my heart rate up just to feel alive, so I was like Forrest Gump, running everywhere. But it was also an immersion, a moving meditation. The full emotions were now flowing through me but I still felt most safe to express those feelings when I was alone. The natural world welcomed me with her open arms and it was there that I would do my work. While having company was pleasurable, it did not allow me the same gift of expression. I had to be alone. I would follow the same paths all the time, both in the conservation land around Weston and on Naushon, and whenever I broke through the pain, its absence made me realize how much pain I'd been in. I found that counting my breaths gave me comfort, reminding me not only that I was alive, but that time was moving forward. Recovering alcoholics use the expression "One day at a time." I began to tell myself, "One breath at a time. Just keep breathing."

Breathing is the key to life, of course. You stop, you die. But try as I might I still couldn't take a full deep breath. Often the air would catch in the back of my throat and I would have to consciously pull it in. Then I would feel it entering my lungs, but in staccato fashion. I was desperate to peel back the layers of scar tissue that seemed to be binding my lungs and making this natural process forced, artificial, and restricted.

Awareness of the breath is also an essential part of yoga, so I went back to my practice, determined to breathe in the air I needed to heal myself, and to breathe out the pain of the grief that had buried itself in every cell of my body. I imagined the air coming in and encircling the pain, and then like a wave slowly eroding a sand castle, swirling back around with the exhalation, retracing its steps but taking some of the pain with it and slowly easing open those doors that had slammed shut inside of me so soon after Charlotte's death.

Through yoga I was uniting the mind and body in the same meditation, and more than one time I found myself weeping through an entire flow class, a full hour with eyes closed, envisioning Charlotte. Sometimes in *shavasana*, the period of quiet rest at the end of each session, I could feel her lie on top of me and comfort me. It was as if the warm blanket of her soul would wrap me up and soothe me in those cherished moments of blurred floating between my world and hers.

I even went on to take a chakra-cleansing class. According to various Eastern healing traditions, chakras are energy centers within the body, sometimes thought to be aligned with the endocrine system. All I know is that emotional pain manifests itself in physical pain, and I needed to attack it from all sides. I found a great instructor, and with her soothing voice to guide me I could feel the energy shifting through my body.

With my newfound access to Charlotte, I started talking to her out loud, a lot, and sometimes the topic of our conversation would be utterly ridiculous, like asking her to help me find a parking spot. I was no longer talking to my six-and-a-half-year-old daughter but to a spirit guide. Her incarnation as my daughter had come to an end. She was now a spirit guide and a special soul. She contained the essence of Charlotte but no longer the little girl. The little girl part of her lifetime remained inside of me as memory and experience, but we had begun to redefine our relationship. There were and are many times that I ached for that six-and-a-half-year-old little girl who was my daughter in this lifetime, but more and more I came to realize that those yearnings were about me and not about her. Charlotte was on her very own and very wonderful path. She was well cared for. She was looking out for us. We were learning to bridge the gap.

I began to have vivid dreams in which her physical presence was absolutely real. It was like the sensation you have when someone is behind you, but then you look and no one's there.

More and more I saw my Charlotte as an ageless soul—a wisdom being—who knows things that I don't and who looks out for Cabot and Beatrice, Michael, and me.

Michael, it seemed to me, continued to think of her only as his lost six-year-old daughter, the loss heavily tainted by anger and resentment, as well as a sense of an absolute boundary having descended between where she had gone and where we remained. It became clear to me that we were processing our grief in very different ways.

However, as much as I craved the kind of contact Margaret had provided, I no longer felt the need to reach out that way. She had opened the door and shown me what was possible. The experience had made me a profoundly different person, suspending skepticism, opening myself up to a much wider range of beliefs and possibilities. I even wondered if I could develop the kind of intuitive powers that Margaret had.

But the most fundamental thing Margaret had provided was the prospect of being able to move beyond the here and now of grieving and to focus once again on creating some kind of future. It was the Oversoul—the unity—I wanted to find. The here and now reconciled with the hereafter.

One day I overheard a stranger talking about a woman named Alexis who worked not so much as a medium but as an insights and intuitions life coach. With apologies for the interruption, I broke in and asked this stranger if she would be willing to give me Alexis's contact information. Later I found out that she was a big deal, consulting with movie moguls and the Dalai Lama.

Despite my lack of such lofty status, Alexis agreed to help me, and our first contact was over the phone. I made absolutely no mention of a death in the family. Alexis knew nothing about me. The woman who had put us in touch didn't even know my name, much less what I'd just been through. And that blank slate was where I wanted to begin.

I opened the conversation by giving her names and asking for whatever came to mind. Michael. "He's struggling." Cabot. "He has respiratory issues." (This was true.) Charlotte. "I see a little girl on a beach. It's like she's at the world's greatest summer camp. She's very spunky and demanding."

"That's my daughter," I said.

But then there was an odd pause, as if Alexis was having a moment of self-doubt, or trying to avoid saying something hurtful. "But this person is on the other side," she said.

She had passed the first test. From that moment on, she became my coach in learning to live a new life based on a new, more expansive way of seeing.

My second meeting with Alexis was face-to-face, in Weston. I don't know what I'd been expecting, but she surprised me by looking so youthful, in a California sort of way. Alexis was about five foot four, with fair skin and long, thick red hair. But the most distinctive thing about her was her very large, incredibly vivid blue eyes. There was something luminous about those eyes, a quality I'd seen sometimes in the eyes of the best yoga teachers. It was as if their eyes were literally more open, and certainly more penetrating.

It was as if she were looking at you twice as hard, seeing what others couldn't see, collecting data on a whole other level.

We were at the home of the woman who had put us in touch. It was in October, and we sat on a little sun porch in the slanting light of late afternoon, surrounded by the glow of orange and yellow leaves. I had brought a tape recorder, but otherwise it was as if we were sharing a cup of tea.

"I just want to get a sense of you," Alexis said, and for a minute or so she took me in with those otherworldly eyes. Then she began to talk, in a stream of consciousness way, and I sat back and absorbed. Sometimes fragments would be unsettling, as in, "I see you crying in the shower" or "I see Michael slamming a door."

But the most disturbing part of our conversation was when I mentioned wanting to have another child. This was vitally important to me at the time, and my frustration was becoming more and more unbearable. But Alexis's hesitation meant that she did not see it happening. Now, in retrospect, I realize that another child could have been a disaster. We were still far more emotionally fragile than we realized, and our tolerance and patience were way down. It took all that we had to simply get through the day and to try to be good parents for Cabot and Beatrice.

Still, I persisted in the hope, and Michael and I continued to try for about another year. We briefly considered the high-tech route of fertility treatments. But by then, I think, we were coming to realize that we were simply worn out, and that perhaps it was best if we just accepted what was and moved on.

I continued to talk often with Alexis on the phone and to meet with her in person once a year. To me, the phone sessions were sometimes more powerful because of the way she could pick up on what was going on without any visual cues. "Hi, this is Sukey,"

I'd say, and she could respond—accurately—with "You have a stomach bug."

Alexis was a strong endorsement for the intuitive self, and she actively encouraged me to explore and embrace more of this new, nonlinear universe I'd discovered. Which led me to explore how this acceptance of the "otherworldly" might have been carried down through my ancestors to me. Emerson's wife, Lidian, was often referred to as a seer or clairvoyant, so I suppose there could have been a trace of that in my DNA. And the more I read Emerson himself, the more I realized that I could give up the academic parsing of his writings and connect to him, and to his own suffering, intuitively. After all, in the face of his own grief as a parent, he's the one who wrote, "I cast away in this new moment all my once hoarded knowledge as vacant and vain. Now for the first time seem I to know anything rightly." To which he added, "The past has baked my loaf, and in the strength of its bread I break up the old oven."

There was no doubt that I was "breaking up the old oven," testing the boundaries of convention, letting go of any pretense of belonging in the world of spreadsheets and "rational" analyses, and every day I was becoming more and more confident that this new path was the right one for me. I've never been a rigorously logical thinker, but I've always had a strong sense of self, which means that even when my emotions were not accessible, I never wanted to be anyone other than me, and I never engaged in much second-guessing as I followed my own internal compass.

But I also knew that until now I'd still hugged the shores. Since Charlotte's death I'd ventured out into the deep blue, whose waters were not only uncharted but also filled, if not with sharks and sea monsters, then certainly with charlatans. I feared my pain had made me vulnerable, and being exploited by someone under the guise of helping me would be bad enough; what would be truly unbearable would be to find that I'd taken on a gauzy and comforting new belief system only to have it exposed and shattered. I needed more solid facts and validation that the ideas that resonated with me did not just resonate because of magical thinking, consuming desperation, or enduring vulnerability. The steps between curious hopefulness and addressing my quiet desperation were ones that I worried might allow me to be led down the wrong path. And yet I had to have answers in order to absorb the magnitude of the loss of my daughter. Where was my daughter? Who was holding her? Who was tending to her needs? I found too many people willing to gloss over those questions and fast-track to the more ethereal answers: "She's with God." "She's in a better place." Bullshit—next to her mother was the best place. Who was the cosmic and almighty parent who was now entrusted with her care? I was consumed by those questions.

A protective skepticism rose up from the more customary part of my New England heritage and forced me to wrestle with my doubts as I moved forward. I was ineluctably drawn to these non-mainstream ideas, and at the same time forced myself to test them against all the input from my previous education and life experience.

If a belief system is old enough to have become "established," the culture shows it a certain respect even when its claims, measured by scientific standards, are ridiculous. The Virgin birth? The Resurrection? God speaking to Moses, or Muhammad, or Joseph Smith? None of these things makes rational sense, and yet millions of otherwise "rational" people confirm their belief in them every day.

Using the term literally, no one can *know* that "Jesus is their personal savior" or that "God waits in heaven to judge the just and the wicked," because *knowing* requires factual evidence—and yet people say they *know* these things. To get to this point of uncertainty, they've made what Loyola called the "sacrifice of reason" and Kierkegaard called the "leap of faith." (He even went so far as to affirm, *Credo quia absurdum*—"I believe *because* it is absurd.") Much of belief relies on faith and much of faith requires that blind leap. And trust. Faith is a requirement of life. Those who have not been tested perhaps do not know this. But most of the world does know that on some level faith is not elective. We often find faith in our darkest moments, when we have exhausted all other hope and have reached the end of the facts. That does not make the leap of faith or the knowing any less true; it just makes it more accessible to us when we most need it. And perhaps this is what it takes. I became willing to take the leap of faith. In so doing I found what to believe. One can factually verify only so much and then very quickly one needs to accept an idea on faith, completely reject it, or dive in more deeply with questions. In my experience, many people, myself included, move open-mindedly partway down that path and then we get stuck on the questions. Really stuck. So we bail out. I am not sure what the recipe is to move beyond that. For me it has required part blind faith, part intuition, more than a dash of curiosity, open-mindedness, healthy skepticism, and trust.

In the years after Charlotte's death I was presented with enough fact and personal experience to allow my intuitive beliefs and experience of life after death to settle into a form of knowing. That has been enough for me to rest comfortably with her whereabouts (for lack of a better word). I had to know that she wasn't totally gone. And that if she was gone I had to find some level of comfort with what her new address was. Even if I couldn't physically visit her, I craved that level of knowing.

I didn't want to be absurd. I didn't want to sacrifice my capacity to reason. And yet I desperately needed to find the "willing suspension of disbelief" that Coleridge talked about in literature. I wanted to move from belief to my own form of knowing.

It has been my experience that when we allow our minds to grow really quiet, we find that most of the answers we seek are inside of us, and they come from that deep space of knowing. It doesn't matter how we get to the stillness. It can be through prayer, or meditation, or repetitive and fluid activities such as walking, gardening, yoga, or running. But it's the silence that allows us to hear what the Bible calls "that still small voice."

Depending on your belief system, that voice could be God, angels, or a spirit guide, the Oversoul, or your personal intuition. But when you hear it, you *know*.

In this way, I think my search incorporated both aspects of my family traditions: the artistic and seeking (transcendent?) side, as well as the restrained and proper side that has sent generations of young men to Harvard.

Having confidence in the power of what "felt right" to me was much harder when I was young and worried that I didn't belong because I didn't live up to the family's lofty academic traditions. I remember telling Grampa Salt, "I'm just not Harvard material," and his replying rather sweetly, "That's okay. After Harvard I went to business school at Stanford and I thought it was a fine school. You should just go to Stanford, then." My small liberal arts college was clearly not on his radar.

But there were plenty of other rites of passage that had allowed me to feel embraced. In the Forbes family it was not so much about love but about being worthy, which meant being invited to do a task side by side, or being trusted to use the chain saw on your own. In the Forbes family, Emersonian self-reliance meant getting your hands dirty.

In terms of what I believed, then, I was being self-reliant, and self-sufficient. I wasn't asking anyone for money to build a church. And I would freely admit that what I'd come to *know* would not stand up to the rational scrutiny that measured ideas at places like Harvard or Stanford. After the Age of Enlightenment, magic, blind faith, and anything that could not be touched and proved in the objective physical world was tossed out on the compost heap. Science and faith became adversaries of each other and seem to remain so to this day. This Euro-American way of thinking and reasoning has clouded us all such that God and miracles play a diminished role in our day-to-day lives. Hard science and theology are certainly not my strong suits, but I have been shown much since my daughter died that leads me to believe, to *know*, that there is much more out there that cannot be explained by science. But even tempered by the modesty of my own as well as scientific limitations, my new, emerging beliefs felt right to me. I became comfortable with my own form of divinity. It was a hybrid of God and Nature and Humanity. And even with those limitations, they brought me through the worst experience a person can endure.

I was now feeling confident enough to go ahead and submit our blood samples so that our DNA could be tested for malignant hyperthermia. We needed to do this for Cabot's and Beatrice's sakes, but we also needed to help researchers learn more about the condition. If anything good could come from Charlotte's death, we had become committed to pursuing it. In this, certainly, Michael and I were one.

That summer progressed, and the humidity of July drifted out to sea, and then the sunlight became brighter and clearer each day. End of summer in New England is heaven, and the fact that you know the warmth is fading makes it all the more precious. I'd always loved the slow change from beach days to back-to-school logistics and the excitement of a new year. But Charlotte had died on one of those perfect August days, and this summer—the first after Charlotte's death—as the weather shifted I could feel my muscles tense again and my jaw tighten as my body remembered. As is often the case with me, I discovered my emotion by tuning in to how my body reacted. I was tense. Sore. Achy. *Aha*. I must be feeling sad.

Anticipation of the anniversary was the worst part. I wanted to wake up on August 19 and say, "Oh, it was yesterday. Damn . . . I missed it." But I felt an obligation to mark the occasion for Michael and for the kids, as well as for all the aunts and uncles, cousins and grandparents. And I was still concerned about being in denial, even now, so I embraced any opportunity to confront a tough situation and feel all that I could feel.

We held our first "Angel Day," as we called it, with the Bigham and the Forbes families gathering on Naushon to remember Charlotte. Annie was there with her two girls and we set off on a long horseback ride that mercifully took up most of the afternoon. During the long ride I was aware of the sun on my face and the warmth that spread through me when I smiled. This was the first time I authentically had smiled in a year and, though short-lived, it felt like a gift. At six o'clock everyone gathered in front of Mansion

House on the lawn that slopes down to the harbor. There were about twenty of us, everyone wearing pink, along with pink rubber bracelets embossed with Charlotte's name.

As the sun began to go down, we released twenty pink balloons. I felt very much on display, but this time I made no effort to hold back the tears. A jumble of dark emotions, I somehow couldn't take my eyes off those balloons rising up toward the heavens. Even after everyone else had gone in, I had to keep staring into the sky until long after the last of them disappeared. Looking into the pale pink sunset sky as the last of the balloons disappeared into the empty distance, I, too, felt empty. My mind went back to the poem of the sail disappearing and then coming back into sight on the other side and I found myself hoping Charlotte was receiving her balloons now as they came into her view. The image of her collecting her bouquet of pink balloons on the other side gave me enough strength to go back into the house and join the rest of the family in the dining room for dinner.

There was only one step left for me to take, and I dreaded it most of all. The next morning, early, I walked over to the Shore House barn, where the Forbes genealogy is documented on the walls with color-coded lines of descent. I found Charlotte's small card, now with a small red dot in the upper right-hand corner.

Charlotte Saltonstall Bigham.
December 23, 1997–August 18, 2004.

I stood and stared at that label, her recent death confirmed by the red dot, and I felt my throat close up and my lungs collapse. I could not breathe or swallow. Then my knees began to buckle. I staggered outside to the bench nearby that was dedicated to my

Staying strong for Charlotte, with temporary tattoos.

grandfather, and I lay prone on it so that I could feel the hard wood pressing into my womb, looked out over the water, put my head down, and sobbed.

We'd passed the one-year mark, and now I assumed I'd been through the worst of it. We'd been through a full year of life events without Charlotte. Surely getting to the "other side" of grief was just around the corner.

9

Second Autumn

About a week after that twilight balloon release on Naushon, I accidentally ran over Lindy Loo, our beloved Jack Russell, and killed her. Anyone would have been upset, but I became completely unglued. I was hysterical. That's when I realized I still had more work to do, and that I would not be reaching the other side anytime soon.

It was the middle of the day, the kids were at camp, and I'd been doing some back-to-school shopping, and I guess I was distracted and took the corner into our driveway a little more sharply than usual. I felt a slight thud underneath the car, and as I stopped I had the sinking feeling that I'd just run over my dog.

I jumped out screaming, "Lindy! Lindy!" Then I saw her crawl out from under the car like a GI under fire. One of her eyes was bulging out of the socket.

I kept screaming, running around in circles. Maggie heard me from next door and came to the rescue. We were always the crisis family, and she was always the rock. I scooped up the dog in the crook of my arm, held her facedown like a colicky baby, and got back into the car with Maggie at the wheel. I kept her there cradled in my arm with the weight of her body and her beating chest pressing into the palm of my hand. As we drove along I could feel the little animal's heartbeat slowing, and by the time we reached the vet's she was dead.

The vet bandaged her eye so that the kids wouldn't see the mess

I'd made of her. I was sobbing and I couldn't stop. It took an hour or so before I could compose myself well enough to head home. I agonized over how to tell the children about yet another family loss.

I pulled myself together, but when I told Michael, I came unglued again. My reaction was so out of proportion that obviously there was a large element of transference at play. But while I had been hectoring myself to be more expressive of my grief over Charlotte, now I was telling myself to calm down. With the dog, I was acting like the crazy person I'd always feared I'd become. I'd gone from a catatonic stoic in the emergency room to a shrieking hysteric at the vet.

Cabot was particularly upset and insisted on looking under the bandage. (Now, years later, he still teases me with an "eye bulging out" expression.) He also insisted on having a burial with a casket he made from an orange crate and a cross to mark the spot. Our other dog, Bandy, walked around lost for days, looking for her buddy, and we lived in fear that she would dig her up.

We found another puppy right away, but this animal suffered such severe constipation that we had to give her repeated enemas. Eventually the vet said, "This dog's not going to make it." After much discussion, we sent her back and got another one, who— perhaps sensing the madness of our family—promptly ran away. The third dog was Pogo, a male, who agreed to stick around.

As we entered our second autumn without Charlotte, everything was about home and hearth, about circling the wagons and trying to restore some semblance of domestic order. We spent a lot of time just huddled around the fire in our old forge, which was cozy and comforting. There was a lot of TV and bad food, but I tried not to berate myself. If my family lived on pizza and Cheetos for a few months, it wasn't going to leave permanent scars.

Even though I likely appeared a little less ragged around the edges, the second year was more difficult for me, just as Sarah had predicted, and I think part of the reason was that everyone else thought I was over the most intense period of grief, which gave me the space—when I wasn't being observed so closely—to cry more easily. I could truly feel the emotions passing through my body, and sometimes even express them. Fortunately, setting aside the episode with the dog, I never went to the scary places I'd feared I might. Having adopted the view that when a loved one dies a part of their consciousness, their soul, and their ability to communicate remains allowed me to recalibrate a bit inside myself. Charlotte was gone from this world in the physical ways that we knew but in other ways she was still very much present. The black-and-white cleaving of her from our family was no longer there. The physical pieces that remain of Charlotte—the soft impressions of her toes in her sparkly pink shoes, her artwork on the walls, her inventive writing, her ashes—all have become place markers for her time here physically. I also see Charlotte in the identical green eyes of her father, the way her sister moves gracefully through a room even when hurried, and in her brother's shared sense of the absurd. I find new evidence of Charlotte when Cabot confides that he quietly prays to his sister to help keep him safe (and win) before each of his kart races, then often feels her sitting on his shoulders as he drives around the track. And we all see her in the red-tailed hawks that consistently appear at family gatherings.

This knowledge that she is not fully gone has allowed for more of a redefining of our relationship. I cannot call her on the phone, but our conversation can continue quietly. In moments of meditation I feel her comforting presence regularly and have found myself settling into our new dynamic with her as the spiritual guide or angel and me as the child or mortal in need of guidance. Knowing that she is still present has made me feel vastly less lonely, and it has brought a calmness and comfort to my soul that has not left me. It also has highlighted the long thread that connects us all from one life to the next. This has made me want to be a better person, wife, mother, friend, and human being. If our existence is a series of lives and incarnations where we continue to learn and grow, then we're really in it for the long haul. If that's the case, I really want to get it right.

I came to realize that the most important thing going forward was to balance my bereavement for Charlotte with my attention to my surviving children. The one thing I could not do was to let that ongoing love be overshadowed by the sense of loss. Like most parents, I struggled with the balance of attention for each child. On any given day one might get more than the others but over the course of a week or month it should all equal out. I tried hard to keep that balance in my bereavement as well. I would try to not give Charlotte more attention than the others. It was obviously difficult and I doubt I was successful at the beginning, but I did try. My need to escape and be alone in nature continued to be a balancing act. I found myself taking every opportunity to hand the children off to willing caregivers so I could get away. I loathed myself for doing this and yet it was all I could do to survive. But the thought of being an absent mother to my surviving children caused me equal amounts of anguish. There were not easy answers, but at least I was beginning to feel human again, albeit deeply flawed.

We were concerned that Cabot was becoming forgetful and not particularly attentive in class, but was he just a wiggly kid or a kid distracted by grief? When he took the usual age-appropriate standardized tests, he scored above average across the board, but he was off the charts in engineering-related skills such as drafting and spatial relationships. This jibed with his ability to lose himself in concentration whenever he wanted to build something with Legos. This was reassuring, but we were still sufficiently concerned that we gave him some private therapy. After all, he was older when Charlotte died, and the two of them had shared a really close relationship. He saw the therapist for a few months, playing games that encouraged him to talk about his feelings, and after a while he seemed to settle down.

With Beatrice, our primary concern was that she seemed to feel obligated to remain small and adorable, as if her job was to cheer us up. She used to tell me that her name was Charlotte, or she'd say, "I want my name to be Charlotte." Was she just trying on a playful fantasy the way any child might, or was there some underlying pathology? I couldn't tell. I went out of my way to say, "No, we only want you to be Beatrice," and we took her to a psychologist as well. The therapist seemed to think that the comments were just normal make-believe, so we just watched and waited, and in time the issue went away.

When Charlotte's eighth birthday came around in December, Beatrice told me through tears, "I don't remember her."

Concerned as we were about the children's emotional health, we were even more anxious about the prospect of genetic illness. We had just received the DNA analysis of Charlotte's tissue from the specialized lab, and the results were conclusive. Charlotte had suffered from an exceedingly rare anomaly that made her susceptible to nontriggered malignant hyperthermia. When the rest of the family's test results came back, it turned out that Charlotte's genetic error had been passed down on my side. I carried one of the genes, but several have to be in place to trigger the condition.

While Cabot also carried one of the genes, Beatrice had not a trace. Even though my son's chances of being affected were very slim, we began having him wear a MedicAlert bracelet.

Of course, Michael shared my concern for Cabot, but his reaction to the role of genetic destiny in Charlotte's death had a different cast to it. For a man who was an old-school provider and protector, losing a child had always weighed on him as a personal failure. Now, with conclusive evidence of a genetic error, he knew there was nothing he could have done, which seemed to lift some of his despair. Unfortunately, the anger he had been turning inward to fuel his depression didn't disappear. He simply began to direct it outward.

I had been through enough of the grieving process by now that I had made peace with it. I assumed that I was going to continue through certain fairly predictable stages, and that eventually I was going to be okay. This was huge for me in getting through each day and in trying to imagine a future. I had found comfort in Alexis's telling me that my future—in fact, my purpose in life—was going to be about making other people comfortable with the kind of loss I'd suffered. The irony, of course, was that I seemed incapable of doing anything for the person I was closest to, and who needed to be comforted the most.

I was no longer worried that Michael was going to kill himself or spiral completely out of control. He was working more, taking care of himself, and his clothes no longer looked like dark rags draped over a scarecrow.

But seeing him emerge from the depression allowed something inside me to shift as well. I don't remember becoming more emotionally fragile, but I must have. I know I entered into a period of being a little bluer, a little less available. Getting dinner on the table was a Herculean task. Showing up at school functions required a performance worthy of Meryl Streep, as did making love and being a wife. My depression sapped all the enjoyment out of the things that should have been the pleasure at life's core. I spent a good deal of time just going through the motions. Fake it till you make it. I was not a great faker.

I remember my husband turning to me at one point and saying, basically, "Snap out of it!" But I couldn't just snap out of it any more than he'd been able to. I was seriously depressed, but not so much that I couldn't stand up for myself and let him have it.

"It's my turn," I said.

In his defense, he caught on immediately and cut me some slack, but it was only for a while. The truce didn't last.

During this period we went back to visit "the ranch" in Santa Cruz, and it was brutal. I hadn't realized how much of California had crept into my being on a cellular level until I returned. We'd closed on the property just before Charlotte was born, and when I came home from the hospital with her this was the home we came to. It was the same when Beatrice was born. So all the sensory reminders of being a young mother of three came back to me, triggered first by the fog rolling in over the western hills as I arrived at the airport, and remembering how the arrival of that fog brought a rapid cooling and dampening, which had always meant it was time to find three small polar fleeces for bundling up the kids before nightfall.

Just driving up the hill I came undone, because everywhere I turned there were memories of Charlotte: our pond, the grasses, the sweet peas, redwoods, wildflowers. They all brought me right back to our time as an intact family in Santa Cruz. When I smelled the Pacific, I remembered sitting in our living room looking out into the redwood grove as I nursed my ten-day-old baby. I smelled the jasmine and I recalled holding one of her hands as she took her first tentative steps, then stopped to steady herself on the trellis along our driveway, and I leaned in with her as she took in the perfume of the flowers for the first time. I felt the parching heat and looked out at the rolling hills turning brown and dotted with California oak trees and I began to hurt all over. With Naushon I had a forty-year relationship before Charlotte was born. I had never known this place without her. This is the California where we lived when it was all okay. This is where we were when life made sense and was fair and perfect. I had recalibrated and re-created my life in Boston, but here I had to struggle anew with the memory of Charlotte, who was not my spirit guide but my little girl in this lifetime, the physical flesh and blood that for six and a half years was my daughter. I wanted desperately for all of life to feel the way it used to feel: warm, cozy, safe, beautiful, carefree, but it still didn't feel that way at all. I walked into her bedroom and my eyes immediately filled with tears. Trying to hold back the sobs, I walked outside to look for Michael. I found him talking to the caretaker and told him, "I cannot breathe. We have to leave right now."

When we returned back east, I felt that it was very important for us to go to church. I did this out of some pretense that perhaps the religious structure would be good for all of us, but I was the one who had to drive the process, which made me the one who was running around the house Sunday morning saying, "Get dressed, comb your hair, tuck in your shirts." And then I would weep through the entire service and count the minutes until I could take a walk in the woods behind our house. We went to St. John's, the same church where we'd had Charlotte's memorial, and though none of us ever acknowledged it, we always avoided the pews where we had sat that day. Michael didn't want to be there, but I wanted to face it all, to go and face it and cry or at least try. I also secretly hoped that being in the church of his faith would awaken some sense of peace in him. This further self-punishing continued for more than a year, and despite all my tears I never once trusted that I was doing it right.

Sharing grief with a partner is complicated. I believe that, for Michael and me, grief changed our views of the world in rather opposite ways. Michael was angry at God. Charlotte's death was unjust and wrong, so God had failed him. I watched as the husband I had always considered religiously devout seemed to turn his back on faith of any kind. The only thing we shared was the view that some higher power had determined that it was Charlotte's time to die.

We each had come into this grief carrying our own baggage. We used whatever tools we had in those bags to patch, rebuild, and pull ourselves together. We expressed our thoughts of feeling lonely and isolated to each other, but we became strangers. We were careful not to condemn each other, but we were both walking alone during a dark time. We remained loyal and true to each other, but we were slowly drifting apart. I interpreted Michael's distance many times as disapproval and perhaps he felt the same about mine. His more classic and visible displays of anguish underscored my fears of inadequately expressing my own emotions.

Increasingly, my sanctuary and my growth came through the daily practice of yoga and time spent in active movement outdoors. Many times I wanted to be angry at God, too, or to blame someone, and yet each day I found reassurance in the warmth I saw people showing to me and to each other, and it made it difficult for me to believe that God was entirely unjust. I took vicarious pleasure in other people's joys, and the desire to bring joy back into my own life took stronger hold in me. Smiles crept back into my daily life and I found myself laughing more easily.

On the other end of the spectrum, we also felt that we owed it to the kids to go to Disney World. The kids loved it. I, on the other hand, found it all terribly fake and contrived, and I was astounded by how much the contrivance ate at me. The music and the smells assaulted my senses, but mostly I just could not tolerate the insistent cheerfulness. Normally I'm an upbeat person, but I found myself wanting to kick each and every "Cast Member" who kept greeting us with "Have a magical day!" More obsequious elves. *Ugh!* Whenever they uttered that focus group–tested mantra, I had to bite my tongue to keep from yelling back, "Don't you tell *me* what kind of day to have!" I was in a bad way. The only thing that got me through it was seeing the smiles on my kids' faces. That, and the adrenaline rush of the roller-coaster ride I shared with Cabot.

Michael loved the manicured perfection and the way it was maintained and run as a business. Oddly enough, he seemed to find "The Happiest Place on Earth" perfectly calming, as if we were strolling around the lily ponds at Giverny. It was becoming increasingly clear that we were developing two fundamentally different approaches to living. He seemed perfectly content to accept the theme park illusions. I couldn't help but see the electrical stations and trash receptacles behind the fences. And like Truman in *The Truman Show*, I never could accept that a painted scrim was actually the sky.

We had already let go of the idea of having another baby, but now we also gave up on the notion of tearing down the house and rebuilding on the same site. I was exhausted just thinking about the logistics of finding a temporary home, then managing such a huge project with all the permitting and legal complexities. Then again, this was the address we'd just moved to when Charlotte died. There was a huge pall of sadness over the place, so maybe it was a better idea to move on.

The solution we chose was to sell the house and buy another one just around the corner. The structure itself was somewhat institutional in appearance, which did not thrill me. But at least this house required only "cosmetic" remodeling, and Michael and I tended to agree on houses and design, so we thought redoing a place would be less stressful for us than for some couples.

We were able to live in the house at the same time, and I found the investment of time and energy to be a welcome distraction. Managing the project, interacting with people, and developing relationships with suppliers allowed me to get out of my head and regain much-needed confidence. It also fed my creativity. For a while it even gave us the illusion that we were getting a fresh start.

Afterward, everyone who saw how we'd transformed the place loved it, which gave me a boost that also became a professional springboard. People began asking me to consult on small design projects. I started a slightly eccentric, definitely eclectic business of finding antiques and other furnishings that I liked and passing them on to my friends. In retrospect, though, I see that the projects were also an emotional dodge to conceal the strains that were beginning to overtake the marriage.

Trying to stay busy was constructive, as was trying to be creative. But I think my most fundamental need was still to be surrounded by all the life I could get. Messy, squirming—it didn't matter. Just life.

In March we took Cabot and Beatrice to Naushon for the lambing. We helped with the deliveries, counting the newborns and bottle-feeding them. It was nippy that time of year and Mansion House had no heating to speak of, so we stayed in a small cottage right in the center of the farm. The connection to the land and shepherding these new lives from womb to our world was life affirming and deeply tender, which was exactly what I needed. We all left rosy cheeked and full of life ourselves.

That spring we allowed our dogs to breed, and soon three puppies joined the household.

Shortly thereafter we added chickens. I ordered a dozen hatchlings through the mail, and they sent eighteen. The local postmaster called and left a message on our anwering machine: "Mrs. Bigham, you have a parcel that's making a lot of noise." I went over to pick them up, and for the next three weeks they lived under a heating lamp in the basement. I found them utterly enchanting and I watched them obsessively. These were healing moments for me. It was about not wallowing, but about being positive, about trying to create a future.

Even when I was feeling numb or struggling with overwhelming emotions, I could always see that it would get better somehow and that I'd eventually find some sort of higher ground. I would carry this loss and it wouldn't break me. Maybe it would become a part of me, and, as Julian Barnes wrote in *Flaubert's Parrot*, I would "come out of it, that's true. After a year, after five. But you don't come out of it like a train coming out of a tunnel, bursting through the downs into the sunshine and that swift rattling descent into the

Channel; you come out of it as a gull comes out of an oil-slick. You are tarred and feathered for life." I'd become strong at the broken places. I was definitely looking to find some kind of mastery over the devastation I'd been through, and determined not to be battered down. I was determined as well to make the most of whatever nuggets of wisdom I might gain through suffering, maybe even use them as mortar for rebuilding. Gaining wisdom and perspective was a compensation I would gladly do without if it meant having Charlotte back, but it's what they call the gift of the loss.

During this period it became obvious that my Saltonstall grandfather was entering his last days. Thanks to Margaret and Alexis, I'd become entirely comfortable with the idea of "crossing over," and that was mostly because I was firm in the belief that you don't really go very far. In Kübler-Ross's terms, dying is only moving from one house to another, like a butterfly leaving a cocoon.

In the spring of 2008, I spent hours upon hours and days upon days at my grandfather's bedside, wanting to be there for him, but also enjoying his company immensely.

"I saw Aunt Sue the other day," Grampa Salt told me. This was my grandmother's sister, who had predeceased my grandmother by seven years.

"Really!" I said. "What was she doing?"

He described how she'd come and visited and talked about people who were already on the other side. This sort of conversation happened routinely as he lingered through his last days.

He was at Carleton-Willard Village, the care facility he had shared with my grandmother until her death three years earlier. His bed was surrounded by watercolors they had done while traveling after his retirement. His wall was a catalog of images that captured all their favorite places.

We talked about memories with him on both sides of the family, and we spent a great deal of time talking about the log cabin that we all loved so much up in New Hampshire. The cabin wasn't a private island, but for me there was the same elemental connection to the clan, and to a particular place. In the 1930s, my grandparents had gone in with some friends to purchase ten acres in Jackson, New Hampshire, and built two small log cabins on Black Mountain. Each of the cabins is roughly twenty feet by thirty feet with a ladder to a sleeping loft that takes up half the space. There are four windows and a door, a wood-burning stove, a long pine table in the center of the room with two long benches on either side, and then the perimeter of the room is beds that double as seating. There are two bookcases with odd items in them and a two-burner portable propane stove. There is no electricity and no running water. It was referred to as "the Palace" in our family.

When I was a child we would all arrive en masse just after Christmas, Mum and her siblings with all of their children in tow, and there would be a scramble for beds. If there was snow we would have to wear snowshoes and/or shovel a walkway to the cabin from the road, which was about two hundred yards, to start our unloading. This would be after a three-hour car trip that would culminate with the children getting out and piling on the bumper of the rusted-out Volvo to provide traction for the last quarter mile of steep hill to our house. Extra traction, Yankee style.

First thing in the morning, my grandfather would turn up at breakfast and announce that anyone who was ready in ten minutes to ski the first run down with him (we lived at the top of the bunny slope) would get their daily ski lift ticket paid for by him.

The great thing about Black Mountain was that we never got lost and yet, as on Naushon, we had a sense of complete freedom.

We would ski alone or in small groups all day. Often we would meet in the afternoon for a multigenerational slalom race. Uncle Jim always won, and I remember how the year my brother finally beat him there was a real sense of passing the torch. The bittersweet feeling of that day was palpable to me even as a blasé teenager.

As a teen, of course, I was incredibly image conscious, and when I deigned to ski with my parents I was mortified by the way we all looked, decked out in "high Yankee," which meant hand-me-down snow pants that were either two sizes too small or four sizes too large. My first several pairs of ski boots had been lace-ups, and my first pair of skis had been wooden with tips on both ends with clip-down bindings made by a relative and discovered by my mother in our basement.

At Black Mountain the ski lifts closed down at three forty-five p.m. and anyone who had missed the last lift up had to hike up the mountain in ski boots with all of their ski gear. There was no phone at the Palace, and even if there had been we would never have dared call. Those long climbs home were exhausting and we made good and sure to not miss that last lift.

At night we'd take turns stuffing newspaper and horsehair into the drafty spots where the freezing air blew in, listen to the mice scurrying about, then sleep in subzero sleeping bags with ice forming on the nails that held the roofing overhead. We would wake, if we were lucky, to a few remaining coals in the woodstove and a temperature in the cabin above thirty-five degrees. Bathroom trips to the outhouse in the middle of the night were to be avoided at all costs.

That cabin was the opposite of Mansion House grandeur, yet I routinely meet people my parents' age or older whose faces light up at the mention of it. It's a bond that can be shared across four generations. It's all about continuity and what's really important in life. Simplicity. Love. Connectedness.

I thought about these things as my grandfather lay dying, my mother and I sitting by his bedside and reading from the journals kept by his mother-in-law. She was a poet, and once a year she would write love letters to each of the children. There were long passages about my grandmother and her relationship with the young man who was now ninety-eight and fading fast. He was utterly still, barely breathing, and many times I thought he might have slipped away. But then I'd watch the corners of his mouth twitch into a fond smile of remembrance.

I've come to the conclusion that the soul knows when life is about to end, and it prepares. It's as if life on earth is a school you have to go through in order to pass certain tests and learn special skills. As soon as you master the lessons you're allowed to go home, to graduate. The greatest of these lessons is unconditional love.

It was very important for my own process to be there to help my grandfather make his transition. His spirit was trapped in a body that had worn itself out after ninety-six years and I just couldn't feel bereft about his passing.

On another night, very near the end, my mother and her brother Jim and I were all sitting with my grandfather. We pulled out our cell phones and called his other two children: my aunt Sukey and my uncle Bob Junior. We dialed them in, put the phones on my grandfather's chest, and then we sang campfire songs, sailor songs, and rounds. Everyone should be so lucky to die this way. This is what the experience of dying should be. It should not happen to a terrified child in an emergency room at the age of six.

I could tell that, being the patriarch, Grampa Salt was worried about leaving his family behind, but in quiet moments I would

whisper to him that it was okay. I just knew he was going to be reunited with his wife and all the people he loved. My experience
within the last several years had given me assurance that he would be
bathed in the white light and folded back into the arms of someone
he loved. His passing would be hard for us, but wonderful for him.

Having a child on the other side, I'd begun to look at deaths in
the family as simply more loved ones gathering around Charlotte.
I was actually comforted by the thought of him joining her. Now
she would get to hang out with Grancy and Grampa Salt.

"You go find Charlotte and tell her I love her," I told him, "and
I love you, too." It took me my whole life to be able to say "I love
you" to my grandfather. Being able to comfortably tell him those
words was a gift to me.

He gave death a few touch-and-gos, and then he was gone.

At the memorial service I thought about all the changes I'd
been through on my own, with Margaret, and then through my
ongoing work with Alexis, and how all of these underscored my
sense of belonging to a tribe, as well as my sense of belonging in
the natural world.

In the eulogy I gave I described how connected I'd always felt
to my grandfather when I was small, and how he used to take each
grandchild out individually and plant a tree in his or her honor.
And then I talked about the raspberries he grew and all the time
we spent in his garden, eating raspberries until our bellies would
hold no more. Over the years he'd given out cuttings so that each
of us could have Grampa Salt's raspberries in our yard.

In the third year, Michael and I began to wear our new identities
as grieving parents in a more permanent way. If that's what they
mean by a "new normal," then I guess this was it.

I was able to look a bit more outside myself, which was particularly important where the children were concerned. I was trying to be more energetic, more creative, more there.

One of the healthiest things we did during this period was to set up the Charlotte Saltonstall Bigham Fund. The idea was that, once each year, we would get together as a family, try to place ourselves in Charlotte's shoes at whatever age she would have been, and then make contributions to causes we thought would have appealed to her. It was a way to keep Charlotte near and, as a family, to explore how she might have grown or evolved as a person. The motto was "Through the eyes of a child, making the world a better place."

Every fall we'd take the kids to a street fair for nonprofit organizations sponsored by the Boston Foundation. We'd let them see the presentations by the various groups; then we'd bring them home and say, "What do you think?" We really wanted Cabot and Beatrice to stay in touch with their sister, so we put a great deal of emphasis on their opinions.

With their input, we decided to support Urban Improv, which visits local schools to perform vignettes typical of the kinds of problems teens face every day, issues like abusive relationships or how to cope with the pressure to do drugs. Another group we helped was Artists for Humanity, which teaches painting and sculpture in inner-city classrooms. We also donated to the Max Warburg Courage Curriculum, a national curriculum and essay contest in the schools that Stephanie had set up in memory of her son.

Stephanie also asked me to serve as one of the judges to read the essays by these kids from challenged backgrounds describing where they had found courage in their own lives. This was an incredibly inspiring, "pull yourself up by your bootstraps" moment for me, challenging me to find my own form of courage. We may have given Stephanie's foundation a little money, but by becoming involved, I was the one who received the gift.

When it was time to raise more money for the Charlotte fund, I turned to several of my friends and said, "You know, we've sat through so many of our kids' dance performances . . . Maybe we should make them sit and watch us." So we created the Yummy Mummy Dance Troupe and began planning a tongue-in-cheek recital fund-raiser.

Beatrice had been taking a hip-hop dance class at a local college, and we hired her teacher to try to whip us into shape. The mothers' dancing ability varied from okay to really abysmal, so we offered a certain price point that would entitle contributors to not show up. You could also pay extra for a seat near the back. The cheap seats were right in front.

This was the first publicly fun and yet poignant event we'd done related to Charlotte. It was our coming-out time—a big milestone. There was some frivolity—everyone wore temporary tattoos that read "Charlotte." We even rented a mechanical bull for everyone to ride.

Michael was the only one to speak, and he did a lovely job. He was very composed, expressing himself with clarity and a soft bit of humor, as if he were presenting at a business conference. I was proud of him, because I knew that, even though I'm a ham and not a bad public speaker, I never could have done what he did.

The dads from Michael's initial therapy group had continued to get together, and he helped turn their casual association into a national organization called Fathers Forever, committed to helping men through the grieving process. This desire for service to others came from a genuinely good place, and in fact I was envious of his ability to see outside himself in grief and to extend his concerns to the community. In this instance, as in every other, his preferred way of helping others was through mentorship.

It was about this time that we added the pièce de résistance to our new house. It was a mural we'd commissioned a friend to paint that ran the entire length of the front hall ceiling from north to south, re-creating the exact configuration of the constellations in the sky over Palo Alto, California, on December 23, 1997, the night Charlotte was born. (We'd checked with the U.S. Geological Survey to get the data.) This was our way of bringing our absent daughter into our new home. We added other symbols that had meaning for us: the hawk that had come to us just after she'd died, barn swallows, and even a few gophers for Charlotte the "critter catcher," who had always enjoyed setting and emptying the gopher traps with Michael. We also had the signs of the zodiac for each member of the family.

I felt I was finally coming out of the darkness. But the stronger I felt, the more it seemed to me that Michael was determined to hold me back. I had begun to smile more and was really feeling the life coming back into me, and yet at times it seemed as if my husband just could not stand to see me happy. More and more I found myself bristling against his persistent small insults.

What I came to realize was that, as I was emerging from the shadows of grief, I was also emerging from his shadow——the kind that's often cast by a very dominant successful man, and with whom I had been unconsciously colluding. This came out in uncomfortable ways——with belittling remarks to me, such as, "That's sloppy thinking." More often, his hostility was more subtle——little things like "forgetting" to return my calls or making sarcastic remarks to me and, upon hearing that they had hurt my feelings, telling me that I was oversensitive and he had been teasing.

Our marriage was under definite strain, and I know I played my part, too. I failed to fully accept his process. I did not embrace his vulnerability, and I pushed it away because it was too threatening to me. I was afraid that it might expose me too much. In hindsight, I admire his ability to allow himself to fall into that deep crevasse without any hint of knowing when or if he would emerge. I was too fearful to do that, afraid that I might never come back.

What if I came unglued? What would the children do without their mother to care for them? How would we function as a family? Worst of all, I was mortified at the thought of my loved ones abandoning me if I truly spoke from my core and said, "Help. I need you." In that I was very much like my father.

When Michael seemed to turn on me, I was afraid he would pull me to that scary place but not be there to help me out of it. I knew that what little was left of me would crumble in that circumstance. I emotionally checked out on him and I'm ashamed of that, and filled with regret for what that must have done to him. Yet the growing tension in our marriage increased my need to protect myself from the new wounds.

Perhaps some of the anger he directed toward me came from a feeling that I was emotionally bailing out on him. But as is so often the case with a relationship, any analysis becomes a bit of a chicken-and-egg problem. All I know is that after a while we both failed each other in our inability to be together lovingly and without judgment.

Our two years in Santa Cruz, as well as our relocation to Boston, had been about Michael's reorganizing his work life to make more time for the family. He made what he considered a noble gesture, done something he considered a sacrifice for home and hearth, and then almost immediately his child died. I think this is how the feeling of such an intense betrayal by God crept into his grieving. He blamed God, but what I wondered was, did he blame me? His emergence from depression came on the heels of Charlotte's test results, but then so did his conspicuous anger. And there was no denying it—the genetic error had been on my side of the family.

In reality, I don't think Michael ever really gave up his desire to be at the top of his field, such that his devotion to family created a tug-of-war inside of him. He worked hard to be present, to be hands-on with the kids, but at any moment he would retreat into his spreadsheets. Michael had always had a challenge integrating head and heart, and Excel had been his way of getting his head around anything, including his emotions. Now he took that approach to his grief.

There were still times when he could be connected and kind, of course, and when he was "on" he was at his feisty and charismatic best. We would all bask in his glow and laugh endlessly at his limericks and funny jokes. But the droughts between our good times, when we were relaxed and connected, became more and more protracted. The good times, and the good behavior, seemed mostly reserved for when others were around.

I really loved Michael. He had always been my first priority and more times than I care to remember I had even put him before the children. Committed to working through these challenges and back to our solid marriage, I could only hope that his remoteness was a reaction to grief. The only thing I knew for certain was that I couldn't win. I got the message from him that, when I was feeling numb, it was because I didn't love Charlotte enough. When I was depressed, he told me to snap out of it. When I was being strong and upbeat, he seemed to resent it terribly. After a while, I couldn't help feeling that he just didn't want me around. But I was determined not to have a divorce be part of Charlotte's legacy.

I'd already given up on the previously most important man in my life. I'd spent more than half my life worrying about my father, but then, in 1996 or so, about the time when Cabot was born, I reached the point where I said, "I'm done." After Charlotte's death, though, he began pressuring me to come visit. I'd lost a child and still had two others to take care of, as well as a husband who was being very difficult. Why couldn't dear old Dad get on a plane to come see *me*? But the guilt continued to accumulate, and eventually I relented and bought a ticket for North Carolina.

My father was in his late sixties at the time, but he looked like he was a great deal older. He had spent the last twenty years or so drinking, smoking, and making choices in his life that seemed to me as though he were working to destroy himself. When I arrived for my visit, he could barely walk. He said he wanted me there so that he could see how I was doing, which was endearing, but it felt very much like a command performance and I was exhausted from keeping up appearances.

I stayed for only two nights, and I alternated between being worried about him and resenting having been summoned for a visit.

On the way home, I was boarding the plane and being very careful as I folded my coat and put it in the overhead luggage compartment. It was a green quilted barn coat with two large pockets. These pockets were made for carrying horse treats, but I used one of them for Charlotte's angel instead. When I got home and emptied my pockets, the angel was nowhere to be found. It must have fallen out on the plane.

I had carried that token every day for three years, planning what I'd wear to ensure that I'd have a pocket to keep it in. I had gone so far as to have a small pocket for it sewn into the lining of my favorite blazer. I would place that glittering reminder on my dresser at night, then in the morning put it back in my pocket. I always wanted it close to my body. And now it was gone. I was devastated.

10

Memory Road

About three years after Charlotte died, I was helping a cousin organize some family papers at her house in Milton when I came upon a lovely painting of William Hathaway Forbes, the father of Donald, the boy who had died of a ruptured appendix on his eighteenth birthday more than a century ago.

I asked my cousin why the portrait was not next to the lovely one of my great-great-grandmother Edith that was clearly its mate and was prominently displayed in her stairway landing. My cousin replied that she did not like the look in William's eyes because it made her sad. In my case, though, it was the look in his eyes that drew me to the portrait to begin with. I knew that look. I had that look. It was the vacant, "trying to cope, trying to hold your head high and keep bootstrapping along despite indescribable pain" look of a bereaved parent.

I fell in love with William Hathaway Forbes on the day I discovered that painting because I understood him on a whole new level. My cousin told me that if I'd have the canvas restored I could take it to Naushon. It is now featured prominently in the front hall of Mansion House. I look at it every day and it gives me strength.

At the same time, unfortunately, I seemed to be falling out of love with my husband, whose behavior was increasingly bringing back the most difficult memories from my childhood. My father had refused for years to acknowledge his depression or seek any help for it, choosing instead to self-medicate and lay the blame for his problems on others. I had been able to emotionally detach myself from my father—mostly—but Michael and I still had children to raise, and if for that reason alone I wasn't willing to give up. All I could do was be patient, hope for the best, and get on with living. If only Michael could have said, "I'm in bad shape. I'm really going through hell here, and I need your help."

To fill the growing void in our marriage, I started taking on more projects, such as redecorating one of the family houses on Naushon, and then putting more energy into my small business—"Antiques and personal adornments . . . with a twist"—which began to take off.

This kind of enterprise has its high-end venues such as the Armory Show in New York, but it also has its down-and-dirty side, where much of the trading between dealers and designers gets done. One of the leading down-and-dirty venues is a kind of antiques "Woodstock" that takes place three times a year in Brimfield, a tiny town in western Massachusetts. I became a regular. In part, Brimfield appealed to my Yankee sensibility of "regifting," good value, and reuse. But I think I embraced the seediness of it with a special relish as an act of rebellion, like a teenager running away from home.

I also liked the lack of pretension of most of my fellow dealers. I wasn't the bereaved parent at Brimfield, and I wasn't Michael's wife. Here I was just another dealer buying and selling—or "swapping shit," as my friend Charles likes to say.

It's a five-day event in which people come from all over the country with tents and trailers and set up a huge outdoor flea market in a series of open fields along Route 20. To transport my gear to and from Brimfield I bought a truck, which I would drive out, unload, then use as a camper. It was like being on the carnival circuit. I met people who had trained at Sotheby's, but also plenty who drove up from Texas in pickups with gun racks or down from Maine and drank beer for breakfast. Every evening we would sit out together in our lawn chairs and shoot the breeze. This was so *not* Old Money. It wasn't even Bright Shiny New Money. It was borderline kitsch, plain and simple, and Michael hated it, which seemed to make me relish it even more.

I also began horseback riding again, which seemed especially important because it was an activity with absolutely no practical utility other than my own enjoyment. There's a stable at Dana Hall that I had access to as an alum, and once a week Beatrice and I took lessons there. It was fun to be learning alongside my daughter. There's something very grounding and healing about grooming a horse, then getting on its back and riding. Moving through a round of jumps takes great focus, as well as an intuitive connection with the animal. Hitting the jump just right gives you a fleeting moment of being weightless, of being carried safely through danger, that I found enormously soothing. Something bigger than me was taking care of me. Something with a pulse.

More and more my interests were shifting toward the physical and the elemental. Michael and I took the family out west to visit Yellowstone, Yosemite, and the Grand Tetons, and I resumed my annual ski trip with girlfriends that we called Chicks on Sticks. One weekend Cabot and I went to a place in New Hampshire that had an upward-blowing wind tunnel that allowed you to experience the sensations of skydiving, only indoors and just a few feet off the ground. It was the first time he and I had shared a mother-son activity that was just about fun and adventure. We both loved it and learned as equals in the training. I noticed him watching me smile while I was flying in the wind tube, and I saw his face soften.

Cabot and I held each other's gaze and grinned as I tentatively dipped up and down in the tube. I knew he'd been watching both his parents closely. I knew that seeing me move to a more emotionally comfortable place was healing for him.

I had always been encouraged to push the limits a bit when it came to physical risks, with chain saws, axes, and shotguns all basic equipment in my childhood. There was a tiny hunting lodge on one end of Naushon, with no phone, no electricity, and a tiny privy, seven miles from the settled area, where a gang of us would go to spend the night when we were barely ten. "Have fun," my parents would say. "Watch out for the snapping turtles." And off we'd go with two hard-boiled eggs and a wedge of cheese for lunch, a can of baked beans, gorp, and apples for dinner. We would use the pump at the Cove to get our water for lunch and boil water from the pond to drink at the lodge. Time had taken some of that carefree spirit away from me, and now I was determined to get it back.

One rite of passage for me growing up a Saltonstall as well as a Forbes was to ski Tuckerman Ravine on Mount Washington, in New Hampshire. It's a glacial cirque, or caldron—a slope in the shape of a concave amphitheater that's way too steep for a conventional ski lift. I could say that I simply never got around to it as a kid, but in all honesty I was just too scared. In 2008, though, I had been feeling small and fragile, even broken, and I needed the challenge. Tuckerman combined a kind of moral fortitude—overcoming the fear to get yourself up there—and then the physical skill to get yourself back down. This was my way of reclaiming the lost wattage.

My brother and I put together a group that wound up being seven men, all solidly expert skiers, and myself. I made a point of wearing white snow pants and a pink parka in honor of "the eternal feminine," but also in honor of Charlotte.

It was a glisteningly bright day as we made the climb, with Jamie and our cousin Alexander setting a fast pace as we hiked the several miles up, each of us with our skis and boots strapped to our back. When you get to the right elevation, there's still more climbing to bring you over to the run, where the descent averages forty degrees, with lots of fifty-five-degree drops, plus cliffs of twenty-five feet or so that you simply have to ski over. Given those conditions, there's also a very real danger of avalanche, and ten people have died there under piles of snow in the past sixty years.

In my pocket I had Charlotte's prayer card with the Helen Keller quote: "What we have once enjoyed we can never lose; all that we love deeply becomes a part of us." I also kept having conversations with her in my head: "Please watch out for us." By this point in my life, when I prayed, it was exclusively to Charlotte.

I found it reassuring that we had my uncle Jed Williamson along, a professional outdoorsman and the editor of the official record book called *Accidents in North American Mountaineering*. He's climbed McKinley and Everest and run Outward Bound programs. He was the one who'd set up the full army-regulation-style ropes course in our yard when I was kid, and had us walking on a four-inch-diameter oak log with just a rope around our waist tied to a "safety" line above and our encouraging parents fifteen feet below.

All the way up the mountain Alex and Jamie were laughing about stories from childhood, heckling me that I was a wimp and that it had taken me forty years to do this. Peer pressure had never brought me here as a kid, and now my motives were anything but the feeling of pressure. I was eager to embrace all the family rites, and to create a closer bond.

It was so hot climbing that I'd stripped down to a tank top, then whenever the sun went behind a cloud the temperature was well below freezing. Part of the way up it started to snow. I'd underestimated how hard it would be just to get up there.

When we stopped to have some food, there were only five other people at the "lunch rocks," which were strewn with boulders the size of cars. The fact that these had a habit of falling all around indicated that this was not the safest place to sit and eat. I had no appetite, but I knew I was going to need an energy boost to get through the rest of this.

Jed gave us the briefing on what to do in case of avalanche— that is, assuming you have a chance to do anything. Ski to the side; don't try to outrun it. If you get overtaken, swim. If you get buried, try to form a cavity around your head so you can breathe. Then spit so you can at least tell which way is down and which way is up.

We took lots of pictures, my favorite being me biting my nails on one hand and holding up my Blue Cross Blue Shield card with the other. "Here it is, just in case," I was saying.

Tuckerman is a big bowl, with Left Gully and Right Gully and the headwall above and between the two for the truly insane. It's so steep that it curves underneath you, and for long stretches there's nothing beneath your skis but air. Fortunately, there were too many spring rivulets and the headwall was closed.

We hiked up Right Gully, and then my cousin Alex took a step forward and dropped down to his waist.

"Uh . . . guys?" he said. "My foot is swinging in the breeze down below here. I think we're on a snowbridge."

I began to wonder if I'd fully recovered from that death wish I'd been exhibiting a few years back. Certainly I'd lost all fear of dying, and I looked forward to seeing Charlotte again. But now that I was feeling life return to me, I was in no rush.

For a moment we stood poised on the rim of Right Gully, and I was thinking to myself, "I've made a terrible mistake." But there was literally no way out but down, and no way down but to ski. Uncle Jed took off, and then Jamie and Alex. So off I went.

The drop was a blur and a rush of instincts, more euphoric than terrifying. In only a few heartbeats I was down and I was alive and I had done it! This was the first step on my way toward deeper, more thoughtful forms of courage. I would need to tap into those deep reservoirs to face the decisions I had to make, some with implications far more frightening than the prospect of a broken neck.

That summer, Anne and Harry and their girls came to stay with us on the island. My husband seemed to have checked out. One night at dinner, in the short period before he went upstairs, his anger spilled over, and he managed to insult just about everyone. My sister-in-law took me aside and said, "I want you to know that you're not imagining this. He is being a complete asshole—to you and everybody else." Anne and Michael had always been close, with a mutual respect and friendship quite apart from the family relationship. It was because of this closeness, and because she had been so careful with all of our family in our grief (and even before she'd saved Charlotte's life in North Carolina), that this statement felt like such a lifeline to me. Fearful that I actually deserved his anger, I had not protested enough when it was first directed at me.

My mother also pulled me aside. "Is he being physically abusive?" she asked.

The answer was no, but I was humiliated that our toxicity had been so obvious. I worried about the kids, concerned about the message Michael's behavior was sending to my son about how to treat women, and to my daughter about what she should be willing to accept.

The next afternoon, Cabot, Beatrice, Michael, and I agreed to meet at the dock, converging from different parts of the island to go for an ice-cream run to Woods Hole. But when I got there, they were gone. Yes, I can be late sometimes, but suddenly there was zero tolerance. Zoom. They'd left me behind. My repeated calls to his cell phone brought no response.

I just sat there—not angry, not outwardly emotional at all. I was simply filled with disgust.

For the next hour I sat in an Adirondack chair by the boathouse, looking out over the water. For the very first time I asked myself, "What do I really want?" Michael had been a wonderful man when I married him, but he was becoming impossible to live with— whether because of his grief, or because of me, or because of something unknown and unknowable. I had to ask: "Am I in or am I out?"

But then I thought again what a terrible disservice it would be to Charlotte for her parents to toss away their relationship. Nobody in the world knew the pain of losing her the way Michael and I did. Our shared sorrow was the ultimate bond. So by the end of that hour I had recommitted to the idea that our shared grief was something that was going to galvanize us rather than pull us apart. I'm his partner, I told myself. I chose him and he chose me, and we're going to find a way to make this work. It just isn't going to be on the terms that it's been in the past.

I was still on the dock when they pulled in. I didn't want the kids to see me screaming. I wanted them to see me being confident and in control. I tried to be very clear with Michael without giving the kids any inkling of just how upset I was. I simply looked at him and in a very calm voice said, "That was really unkind." Then I dropped it.

My husband may not have understood my reaction, or the importance of the exchange, but this was a huge turning point for me. I was done with crying and showing weakness to get him to respond from a position of superiority. That was the old road, and I was not on it anymore. The path forward required me to actually acknowledge my own power and independence, my will, the value of my own responses and feelings, and to act on those things.

From that moment on, my high-achieving husband was still my husband, but he was off the pedestal, a shift that upset the basic premise of our relationship. As time went on and the remaining bond continued to unravel, I worked less hard at nurturing what was left. When Michael would sit in stony silence for days on end, communicating only through text messages or spreadsheets, I made no effort to pull him back in. I had given up being the sole caretaker of our emotional connection.

My preoccupation was shifting further away from grief and more toward fashioning a future that would be best for me and my surviving children. I was determined not to let the marriage fail, but I was also determined to stop catering to his every whim. I'd already given all I had to give. To survive, I had to become a neutral country, like Switzerland. We could still make this work, I felt, but he was going to have to meet me at the border.

Yoga had been helping me reconnect with my physical reality, helping me get out of bed each day and see the beauty of the world. Now in my meditations I began to focus on my third eye— the "brow chakra," or inner eye, that true believers say is the portal through which enlightenment can enter. It's also a symbol for what one Christian mystic called the "naked and undefended now." All I knew was that it stood for the merger of intuition and reason, sensory input and reflective intelligence, and I liked the sound of that.

Ever the daughter of a sailing family, I thought of the third eye as a porthole through which I could peek out. Sometimes I would visualize pulling items or people in through the portal to keep them close. Other times I would push emotions or thoughts or people out. Eventually, I would see it as a portal through which I could escape and just keep running.

I tried sitting meditations and I struggled with staying focused, but the flowing movement of yoga seemed to allow my mind to free itself. So I made it a daily practice, and I planned my days around my sessions on the mat. The children were in school during the week, but weekends were more challenging. On weekends I alternated between missing yoga and feeling resentful, and going to yoga and feeling as if I were neglecting my family. But I was noticeably more calm and at peace when I made it to class.

That fall I was out hiking in Arizona with a group of girlfriends. By this time I was no longer being preintroduced with the hushed "You know she lost a child . . ." I no longer felt I had to share the information in the first sentence of discussion with acquaintances. On this trip we were all on vacation and feeling good and being completely goofy, laughing and taking turns doing yoga poses on the tops of rocks along a trail. Another hiker was passing by and he stopped to watch us. After a moment, he pulled aside one of my friends and asked her about me. "Has she lost a child?" My

friend was dumbfounded, but said yes. Then this stranger said
that he was a medium and that he was hearing from my little girl.
He said he simply wanted to pass along her greetings, and to say
that she was doing well and was happy to see me so happy.

This sort of visitation or message happened to me with in-
creasing frequency now. My experiences with Margaret and with
Alexis had opened up the doors to perception, and once the senses
were awakened, the reinforcement just kept coming. My whole
concept of everything—the boundaries between the natural and
the supernatural, between the living and the dead—had been
transformed.

None of this would make the least bit of sense to Michael. He
and I were still trying to hold it together, but from the outside, as an
act of the will. The inner core that makes a bond seem natural had
begun to dissolve in our very different responses to grief. The fact
was that through a shared experience we had followed very divergent paths. Michael, it seemed, had lost his old faith, while I had
found a new one. In the immediate aftermath of Charlotte's death,
when it was all we could do to lick our wounds, the experience had
bound us together. But now, as we came stumbling out of the haze,
we were emerging as completely different people.

As my bond with Michael faded more and more, I felt myself
drawn more and more to exploring my bonds with my family of
origin.

For someone for whom the embrace of a Boston Brahmin family
was so important, the alternative beliefs and practices I was drawn
to could have been problematic. But as I began to shake the family
tree a bit more, increasingly I found that I was in good company.

I moved beyond my great-great-great-grandfather Emerson's

ideas to how he conducted his life. I felt a glimmer of recognition when I discovered his relationship with Jones Very, the certifiable madman who got booted off the Harvard faculty, then locked away at McLean when he claimed to be the Second Coming of Christ. My great-great-great-grandfather edited Very's poetry and became his champion. He didn't mind that the man was a lunatic. Neither did my great-great-great-grandmother Lidian.

At the same time, I found myself growing less and less accepting of Emerson's treatment of his wife. Ralph Waldo may have been the famous one, but Lidian was my ancestor as well, and it bothered me the way he marginalized her and how she lived in his shadow despite the fact that she wrote her own essays on Transcendentalism and the fact that he incorporated many of her ideas into his work. He had wooed her under the pretense that she was going to be an intellectual partner, and she had subjected him to a two-hour interrogation during which she made it very clear that housekeeping and domestic affairs were not her strong suit. She had wanted to be very clear about how he viewed her, about her future role as a wife, a mother, a life partner, and she would not accept his proposal until she was satisfied with his answers. She was a strident and bold woman of strong convictions, easily her husband's intellectual peer. And yet very quickly their marriage took on the traditional asymmetry she had wanted to avoid.

After the death of Waldo, she spent her days and nights hiding upstairs in her bedroom while Emerson entertained hoards of guests. She even had to suffer the indignity of her husband's near obsession with another woman, Margaret Fuller. In family albums, Lidian's image appears to recede, becoming ghostly and ethereal, as if the sun damage and natural fading of the photographs had affected only her. And through it all Emerson seemed indifferent to her suffering, dismissing it as hypochondria. The height of absurdity was that, early in their marriage, he'd decided that he liked the alliterative sound of Lidian Emerson better than Lidia Emerson, and so he arbitrarily changed her name! She went along with that kind of belittling treatment. In my marriage, I would not.

Delving further into the family history, seeking companionship, comfort, guidance, I discovered that my uncle Eric was an expert on Islamic mysticism, and that my cousin Paula, a devotee of Krishnamurti, had held séances at a Vedanta temple. A cousin from the Emerson Society wrote a book called *Be-ism* (as opposed to atheism), which was essentially a reworking of the Emersonian idea of God as nature and nature as God. (Another family member adopted a hippopotamus when the zoo could no longer care for it and kept it in her grandfather's stable.)

But my interest in the fringier side of the family coincided with a new and more specific interest in the Forbes women as women. I became especially intrigued by my aunt Ruth Forbes, who had always seemed so exotic when I was growing up because she did yoga and lived west of the Hudson River. To my eight-year-old self, she had appeared hopelessly glamorous when she came to our house on Naushon, her long silver hair braided and wound into a bun on top of her head. She obviously cared about her body, and I would get down on the floor beside her as she went through her yoga postures, fascinated by her lightness, by the way she seemed to float.

Aunt Ruth, I discovered, was a pacifist who used her fortune to establish the International Peace Academy and who, in her spare moments, did watercolor portraits of alien beings. Her first husband, Lyman Paine, was a Trotskyite. Her second, Gilbert

Thomas, I don't know much about because he died shortly after their marriage. Her third was Arthur Young, who is a story unto himself.

Uncle Arthur was a brilliant physicist and engineer who developed the Bell helicopter. After Uncle Arthur retired from Bell, he devoted himself to investigating phenomena that mainstream science ignored. "I am interested now in the Psychopter," he wrote, "because it won't work. What is the Psychopter? It is the winged self. It is that which the helicopter usurped—and that the helicopter was finally revealed not to be."

I found this passage reassuring—if only because nothing I could ever come up with would ever sound as nutty as this.

About five years into my grieving process, I decided to look up Arthur and Ruth's son Michael, as well as their grandson Chris. I remembered Chris from my teen years on Naushon, a slightly awkward teen with long hair, always walking alone, emerging unaccountably from the bushes at the strangest times.

With a little bit of digging I found that Chris had started a commune in Sebastopol, California. Later, his father joined in and helped him acquire more land. I remembered my cousin Michael as being slightly older than my parents and having the austere tight-lipped Forbes look that is sort of a genetic maker's mark. When he'd stood up to speak at our annual meetings in August, I'd always been intimidated by him. He was smart, articulate, determined, and even a bit autocratic. But obviously, there was more to that Brahmin facade than I'd realized.

Sebastopol is near Santa Rosa, about an hour north of San Francisco, and on the drive from the airport once again, overwhelmed by Charlotte memories triggered by the madrone and oak and the smell of sage, the tears started. I also began to worry that I was going to have my long-awaited gothic meltdown surrounded by naked hippies and two relatives I hardly knew.

The commune, Green Valley Village, has a long access road. There are cattle poles over the river, and eventually you come to a dilapidated farmhouse surrounded at varying distances by old school buses converted into mobile homes, mud huts, yurts, and platforms in the woods that looked like bird nests, with a gypsy caravan twist. Many had solar panels, and the jury-rigged electrical wires running here and there looked like something Rube Goldberg would have appreciated.

Much to my surprise, cousin Michael pulled me into a very warm embrace the minute I saw him. I hardly knew him, and yet he gave me a wonderful welcome that didn't seem forced in the least, but utterly gracious and heartfelt.

Like my Saltonstall grandfather, Michael is six foot four, and even well into his eighties and despite his recourse to a cane, he has a regal carriage and moves with a purposeful stride.

As soon as we sat down to talk, I described my reason for being there as wanting to learn more about his mother. Within minutes he was telling me that he felt she'd never hugged him enough as a child. It was such a guileless and sweet statement. I could actually feel his pain over that lack of warmth in his early life.

His childhood had been very eccentric, bouncing around with his mother between her first divorce and her eventual marriage to Arthur. He'd lived all over, including once in a miner's hut in Nevada, where he said he had been mesmerized by the sound of the rain on the tin roof. (Hello, Charlotte.) But he'd always taken the train all the way back across the United States each year to spend his summer on Naushon.

Eventually Chris joined us, and we spent a long time sitting in the living room discussing Aunt Ruth, and Michael's not only challenging Arthur on his design for the Bell helicopter, but being right!

In the late forties, about the same time that he married Aunt Ruth, Arthur discovered Theosophy and the teachings of Madame Blavatsky, Zen Buddhism, and Hindu philosophy, as well as the study of precognitive dreams. He and Aunt Ruth took up with Mary Benzenberg Mayer, who had studied under both Freud and Jung. In 1952, they started the Foundation for the Study of Consciousness.

Michael was very animated when speaking about the engineering of the helicopter, even more so when he got around to the application of higher mathematics to astrology. Arthur had spent his later years developing what he called his Theory of Process, a way of unifying consciousness, physics, and biology through calculus and quantum theory. "The universe, far from being a desert of inert particles," he wrote, "is a theater of increasingly complex organization, a stage for development in which man has a definite place, without any upper limit to his evolution. The real function of science is to explore the human spirit."

I was picking up about every fifth word my cousin was using, and after our conversation I had no more precise understanding of Arthur and Ruth's spiritual and metaphysical beliefs than when I had arrived. But the whole point was that I didn't have to understand it precisely—I could feel it. Intellectually, I was a fish out of water; emotionally, I was completely at home.

I nodded my head and gazed out the window. As Michael and Chris continued their discussion, a man with a ZZ Top beard drove up in a beat-up Mercedes. Two bare-breasted women stopped outside the house and had a twenty-minute chat. One of

...ad just returned from a three-day clothing-optional retreat in the woods, and she was so energized from the experience she practically hovered over the ground. Is this what Arthur had meant by the "Psychopter"?

Michael then took us out for a tour of the property, and despite the hitch in his walk, he led us at a fast clip through the dry yellow pampas grass, the eucalyptus trees, the madrone. It was all so much like our place in Santa Cruz that I could hardly breathe. Even more striking, while it was completely different from Naushon, I still felt the same religious awe. Walking through the virgin-growth redwoods, I could feel my past and present coming together, the part of me that had been drawn to California and the part of me that remained wedded to Naushon. I thought of Emerson: "We see the world piece by piece, as the sun, the moon, the animal, the tree; but the whole, of which these are the shining parts, is the soul."

Michael had to get back to the house, but Chris and I went down to the pond and sat on a small dock where a canoe was secured with a frayed rope. We took our shoes off and dangled our feet in the water, and I was struck by the contrast between the cold water and the dusty dry air of the valley. We sat there for a long time, and I told Chris about the connection I felt with Arthur and Ruth. Eventually we got around to all the searching and the metaphysical speculation I'd been engaged in, and I mentioned the idea of "soul groups." Chris was right there with me. "Absolutely," he said. "Moving through life in clusters of individuals. Like a secret brotherhood traveling on the same ship."

I smiled. It occurred to me that maybe now I was officially one of the "crazy cousins," and the thought was liberating. I felt both "out there" and at the same time embraced by the protective warmth of a clan.

I'm too attached to my creature comforts to live on a commune the way these cousins did, but we were all on the same kind of quest. "Build, therefore, your own world," Grandpa Emerson said. "As fast as you conform your life to the pure idea in your mind, that will unfold its great proportions. A correspondent revolution in things will attend the influx of the spirit."

Michael and Chris invited me to attend church with them the next day, which both surprised me and filled me with dread. They hardly seemed like the churchgoing types, and I didn't want to spoil the high I was on by confronting an institutionalized interpretation of God, the soul, and the hereafter.

When we pulled up to the Unitarian Universalist church in Santa Rosa, the utterly nondescript building did nothing to overcome my resistance. We entered through glass doors set in a cinder block building that could have housed the town water department.

The service was already in session, so we sat in the back. The minister was a woman, and I looked around at the sunbaked Californians in their khakis and blue jeans, so different from the Unitarian congregations of my childhood—not a blue blazer in sight. But then, when the responsive readings began, I thought, "You gotta be kidding me." The first was from Whitman's *Leaves of Grass*:

Not I, nor anyone else can travel that road for you.
You must travel it by yourself.
It is not far. It is within reach.
Perhaps you have been on it since you were born, and did
    not know.
Perhaps it is everywhere—on water and land.

This was followed by another passage from Whitman that could just as easily have come from Emerson: "I hear and behold God in every object, yet understand God not in the least."

They were speaking my language.

The minister announced that it was time for a guided meditation. "Right here?" I thought. "In church?"

She led us through a series of breathing exercises, then told us to imagine that we were walking through a meadow. "Feel your feet on the ground, smell the smells, pay attention to all that surrounds you."

I loved this, and I really got into it, feeling deeply moved and yet also on the verge of giggling. This was so *not* what I had expected. I floated around in this meditation smelling all the California smells.

I could hear the minister's voice intrude ever so slightly. "Ask yourself where you should be putting your attention right now," she said.

I asked myself that question.

Immediately, I heard a voice inside of me say, "Be divine."

"Be divine?" I asked myself. "You mean like Bette Midler?"

But then my smart-aleck mind quieted down and I let the message sink in. "Be divine." What does that mean? *Live divine. Find divinity in your life.*

"Okay," I thought. "I can do that. At least I'll try."

The minister gently brought us out of our meditation and back to the literal world of the unadorned chapel in Santa Rosa.

Then, most astoundingly, what should she begin to talk about but being divine—about finding the divinity in everyday relationships, objects, and experiences. My jaw dropped and I put my hand over my mouth to stifle a gasp. It felt in that moment as if

God, whoever or wherever or whatever he or she was, had created that service just for me. Certainly that service on that day spoke right to my soul. In that moment I knew I'd made it home.

After a few more thoughts on everyday divinity, the minister closed the service by putting her hands in prayer position. Bowing slightly forward, she said, "Namaste," the Hindu greeting that means "The spirit within me greets the spirit that is within you."

"Namaste," the congregation repeated.

I had come full circle, and it brought to mind another of my great-great-great-grandfather's observations: "Our life is an apprenticeship to the truth that around every circle another can be drawn: that there is no end in nature, but every end is a beginning."

There I was, in all the divine glory I could muster. I realized that the divinity in life I was seeking would come not only from my new spiritual Brahman path, but from whatever inner wisdom had accrued to me in forty-seven years as a Boston Brahmin. I will be divine. I will trust this. "Trust thyself." Thank you, Ralph Waldo Emerson. I get it.

A week or so after I returned east, Michael, Cabot, Beatrice, and I went over to Nantucket to visit friends and family. Beatrice and I took the ferry from Hyannis, and Michael and Cabot drove our small boat over from Naushon. They planned to drive it back as well, but when the last day of vacation came, high seas and rough weather put a kink in everybody's plans. Michael was due back in Boston for a couple of meetings, and the kids were eager to get home, so they all got a ride back together, leaving me with a seventeen-foot outboard that needed to be returned to Naushon across thirty miles of open ocean. I stayed one more night, hoping the weather might improve. If it didn't, I'd take the ferry back to

Boats in the Naushon harbor on a calm day, 2007.

the mainland myself and figure out what to do with the boat later. A seventeen-foot inflatable, it was moored at my cousin John's place at Brant Point. He told me they could tow it over later if need be, but I did not want to impose on their generosity.

The skies the next morning did not look promising, but then my cousin called again. He said he'd checked the forecast for me and the winds were going to be calm by midday. He thought if I could just wait a couple of hours I should have no problem motoring back to Naushon. John knew all about small boats—he'd commanded one in Vietnam. So when he brushed aside my concerns and said, "Do it," I felt pretty safe. "I wouldn't send you if I didn't think it would be fine," he told me. "And it just might be the highlight of your summer."

John knew I was nervous about the open ocean, and he said he'd help get me going. As he and his wife, Teresa, helped me load the boat, they tried to calm my nerves about the distance and the weather. Sure enough, by the time we got off the mooring, the weather was spectacular. It was end-of-summer "Charlotte weather," and the now familiar wistful feeling was beginning to set in. This was just the kind of adventure Charlotte would have loved. I sent a silent prayer to her to join me on the crossing.

We headed out past the breakwater together, I in our glorified skiff, my cousin in a big thirty-footer with two huge engines on the back. He'd given me a compass reading, and he'd promised to escort me until the Vineyard came into view on the horizon. From there it would be easy, he said, with Naushon tucked in just on the other side of the larger island.

The breeze was gorgeous, the seas were calm, and the two boats were just zipping along, heading out into the blue water. I knew the Cape was to the north and the Vineyard was to the west, and after a while I could see the promised speck of land. John signaled for me to slow down while they pulled alongside. "Just stay on this compass heading and you'll be fine," he said. "Don't go that way or you will hit the shoals." He looked at me and then added with a grin, "You will be fine. I know that grandfather of yours taught you celestial navigation, so if it gets dark you'll be able to find your way as well."

I waved good-bye to them and started off. A couple of minutes later I saw the large and very familiar boat out of the corner of my eye. John was waving me to the right and pointing his long arm like a weather vane. I smiled and nodded and waved again, and once more I took off. A few more moments passed, and then he was alongside again, looking mildly concerned but mostly amused. This sea captain thing was trickier than I'd thought. Go the wrong way and you could just keep on going.

At last my cousin must have been satisfied that I wasn't heading to Portugal, because he fell off and turned around, and I had this moment of "Oh my god—I'm out on the ocean all alone." There were no boats anywhere, and that speck of land I'd seen earlier now seemed rather less distinct.

"So, Charlotte . . . What d'you think?" I said. "Think we can find North America?"

I opened up the throttle and started flying along at full speed, all by myself, the surface undulating in those big ocean swells. My hair was blowing in the wind, and by now any fear had given way to excitement, so much so that the exuberance rose up from the tips of my toes through my entire torso, then expressed itself as a thrilled howl at the top of my lungs. John was right. This was the best I'd felt all summer. This was the best I'd felt in years.

When I got to Woods Hole, I left the boat for a cousin to pick up and ferry over to Naushon. Then I got in a taxi for the forty-five-minute ride to the Steamship Authority dock at Hyannis to pick up my car.

The driver was a chatty Middle Eastern man, and when I got in the car I just couldn't contain myself. I told him all about what I'd just done and he acted suitably impressed. "You are full of courage," he said. But mostly I was just full of myself, feeling ebullient, feeling great. We went on to have a lovely conversation about the summer and the change of seasons and I was like a talk show host, drawing him out, asking him about his background and how he came to be living on the Cape and driving a cab.

When we got to Hyannis and pulled into the parking lot, he turned around to look at me and said, "Your husband is one heck of a lucky man. I hope he really appreciates you because you are just one heck of a woman. And if it doesn't work out, I want you to call me up!"

We laughed. He was a big, fat, bald grandfather type, but he was utterly charming. Then he said, "I had such a nice time talking to you today. You are just so full of life."

I thought, "Wow. He thinks I'm full of life. Am I?" And then I thought, "Yeah. I guess I am."

As I got out of that taxi I felt that every cell in my body was humming. And I said to myself, "Okay. Maybe I'm back."

In 2011, and with great regret, Michael and I decided to pursue an amicable divorce. Now when I go back to Naushon it's just me, or me and Cabot and Beatrice. But each time I go I include a visit to the family memorials hidden in the woods in the Aisle of Beeches.

Up a small rise from the cluster of graves my eyes now automatically seek out the plaque that we placed on the boulder in remembrance of our little girl. I still go up to clear away the vines, and I sometimes take a nap in the cool dirt in front of the boulder and commune with her.

The year Charlotte died, Tibetan prayer flags appeared in the trees above her stone. I have no idea who hung them there, but they've lasted through many winters now. And each season I find little fairy houses made of sticks at her memorial, constructed no doubt by her young cousins. It comforts me to know that, generations hence, she'll be remembered on the island as the beautiful little Forbes girl who was taken by a fever when she was six.

It's hard to know the woman I would be today had I not been utterly derailed by the death of my daughter. Even now I find myself cataloging memories in terms of "before Charlotte died" and "after Charlotte died."

She's been gone longer than she was ever here. The passage of time since her death has not softened its impact, but the years have allowed me to file the wound inside of me so that it does not overpower me on a daily basis. The triggers that bring on the pain are better known to me and I am better able to sit with the pain when it comes. But that doesn't make the pain any less.

On my first visit to her memorial, I realized that this was a place for the living, a place to trigger our memories of Charlotte, and that she shows up only when I show up. Otherwise, at least in my mind, she's at the beach with her friends on some perfect adventure.

I chose to look deeply enough into Charlotte's death to somehow find the gift of the loss. Which is to realize just how much is *not* important in life, and how important it is to let all the unimportant stuff go. And there is so much that is just not important. I often feel like reciting that monologue from *Our Town*, the one in which the young woman given a furlough from the graveyard wants to jolt all the citizens of Grover's Corners into seeing and feeling the beauty of the life they're living every hour of every day.

I still have Charlotte's pigtails in the drawer where I keep the Mass card from her funeral, the autopsy report, and other fragments of her life and her death. Her sparkly pink shoes rest on my desk atop a stack of books. And I still sit there at my desk, going through these things and, yes, grieving. But when I see Charlotte again, I don't want to have to say, "I took to my bed after you died. Losing you just about finished me." Instead I want to be able to say, "Hey, what have you been doing? This is what I've been doing. This is what I learned from losing you while you were still so young."

I don't ever expect to be finished with grieving, nor do I want to be. My main job right now, though, is providing a safe and nurturing environment for my two living children and continue to coparent them well with Michael. I still hold everything that was

Charlotte close, and there is a gaping hole in my heart that I don't expect will ever be filled. It will stay black and it will stay painful. But in compensation for that hole, what I've been able to do is grow my heart larger. The hole is there, but there's more room for life. There is still room for grief even while I'm full of life. Without hesitation I would trade every bit of this newfound zest for my daughter's safe return, but that can't be. Instead I'll stay full of life, for me and for Charlotte, and I'll honor her life by carrying her through mine.

On Naushon, not long after that trip to Santa Rosa and my "rite of passage" boat ride back from Nantucket, I took a walk along Memory Road (that's its name—really). I was looking up at the sky, feeling the sun and wind on my face, when suddenly I was overwhelmed by a feeling of love and acceptance and belonging. The ground I was walking on was my family's ground, and I was feeling deeply embraced by that family. That's when it occurred to me for the first time that it was okay to feel okay. Charlotte was with me, and I was able to share this experience of profound love with her. I kept repeating, "I love you" and "Isn't this magnificent?"

At that moment I realized that I'm no longer even remotely concerned about death. In fact, I look forward to it—not that I'm in any hurry, mind you. But I have a child over there, and family, and lots of other great people. So when death comes . . .

Walking along that island path, the feeling of love and connection so overwhelmed me that I closed my eyes, tilted my face toward the sun, and kept walking, trusting that I knew the way well enough not to break the spell by smashing into a tree. The sensations flooding my body seemed like what all the mystics describe when undergoing their "peak" experiences, whether it's Saint Paul on the way to Damascus, or a Forbes in the 1920s doing "Sacred

Dances" at a guru's château outside Paris, or a hippie Forbes from the sixties sitting in an ashram in India. I felt a complete cleansing—maybe even a rebirth—which somehow needed to be marked and celebrated. This was Naushon, not Galilee, and there was no Jordan River, but Silver Beach was right there. So I stripped off all my clothes and went running into the water, just the way my grandfather David Cabot Forbes had taught us.

ACKNOWLEDGMENTS

A few key people set the tone for my journey through grief and subsequent writings. Connie and Bob Loarie reached out to me via letter and, by sharing a friend's story, offered the only words that brought me solace in the initial months after Charlotte's death. Michealene Cristini Risley, Jackie Speier, Jan Yanehiro, and Deborah Collins Stephens planted the seed in me that was the genesis of this project when they asked me to contribute an essay on my grief experience for their book, *This Is Not the Life I Ordered*. Once I started writing I found I could not stop.

A rich tapestry of extended family on all sides has allowed me the great lifetime blessing of feeling embraced by a clan. I am grateful each day for the legacy left behind by John Murray Forbes. The continued shared sense of stewardship of both land and family has been passed down and cherished in our family now for eight generations. My gratitude is extended to those family members who shared recollections, letters, archival information, and in some cases diplomatic advice: Beatrice F. Manz, Ruth F. Brazier, Ralph Forbes, Tally Saltonstall Forbes, Jim Saltonstall, Paul Elias, Perry F. Williamson, Beth Colt, George Howe Colt, Sophie Morse, David Gregg, Scott Schoenfeld, Eliza Castaneda, and Dan Emerson.

My sister-in-law Anne Savarese, MD, deserves special mention. She saved Charlotte's life the first time and then held our family in her tight embrace after Charlotte could not be saved the second time. By sharing Charlotte's story in her own lectures as a pediatric anesthesiologist she has given a face to malignant hyperthermia and in so doing has personalized the syndrome to more physicians.

The gratitude I feel for my group of readers and friends, some of whom read every draft of the manuscript, each time with a fresh eye, can never be adequately stated. They offered feedback on content, flow, and fact checks, as well as much-needed encouragement. When the going got rough they patched me up with duct tape, tireless listening, big hugs, boxes of tissue, nutritious meals, long walks, wine, milk chocolate, and moral support too many times to count. Thank you, Stephanie Warburg, Tally Forbes, Jamie and Alison Forbes, Beth Colt and PK Simonds, Paul Elias and Marie Lossky, Alex Kerry, Tom Dwyer, Jennifer George, Nicole and Matt Miller, Ralph Forbes, Julia McLean, Nancy Adams and Scott Schoen, Patty and Charles Ribakoff, and especially Kevin O'Leary.

Suzane Northrup and Blair Chymberjehle provided insights into this life and beyond and nurtured in me the ability to further develop my own belief system. Blair's guidance and counsel continue to source my soul. She is an angel on this earth. Yogis Jacque Bonwell, Jordan Lashley, Alexandra Wheelock, and Baron Baptiste watched me breathe, weep, and flow through many of their classes and helped create space inside of me for writing and healing. Namaste.

Marcia Mafra, my secret weapon. She has the most positive attitude and innate sense of kindness of anyone I know. The perfect assistant who always knows what I need before I do and quietly delivers it with a smile. Everyone knows I am lost without her. She makes our life work.

Without William Patrick I would never have been able to thread together all my loose ramblings and recollections into a cogent and readable narrative. He asked all the right questions to bring clarity to the issues and is great company to boot. He is a true friend, the perfect confidant, and a brilliant editor.

Bonnie Solow of Solow Literary, my agent and *new* old friend. Oh, how I won the lottery when we found each other. She called me to higher levels on all fronts and delivered even more in return. Her passion for excellence is unwavering and her capacity for empowering is extraordinary.

My editor at Viking Penguin, Carole DeSanti, along with Viking's president, Clare Ferraro, immediately "got" my story. Carole's pointed but profound questions along the way pulled a richness of story from me that I did not know existed.

Also at Viking, Chris Russell, Carolyn Coleburn, Nancy Sheppard, Paul Lamb, Winnie DeMoya, Rebecca Lang, and the rest of team took me under their wings and helped launch this book. Each brought their A-game and seemingly boundless knowledge and enthusiasm to our meetings.

Mark Fischer did yeoman's work reviewing all legal documents. His turnaround was quick and his wit even quicker.

Susie Stangland and her team, along with Sandi Mendelson and her team at Hilsinger Mendelson, have been a dream come true in their energy and commitment to the promotion of this book.

The Massachusetts Historical Society, Historic New England (formerly SPNEA), and Harvard's Houghton Library provided quiet spaces for research and reading.

Social media is a curious phenomenon and one I have joined only in the last two years. In particular, my Facebook and Twitter network of "friends" has provided feedback, comic relief, inspiration, and a great place to hide while procrastinating. Many of them I do not know personally, and yet through this modern marvel of communication they have become important parts of my process.

I have been blessed with great parents, Tally Saltonstall Forbes and Ralph Forbes, who, along with my siblings, Jamie Forbes, Heidi Forbes Oste, and Laura Forbes Hill, have provided valuable feedback about areas of close- and extended-family sensitivities. They have all been champions of my work and have shown grace in their acceptance of my words in some of the more delicate family sections.

Michael Bigham urged me to take on this project and continued to be supportive despite challenges along the way. Our three children have been fortunate beneficiaries of his love and devotion.

Cabot Forbes Bigham and Beatrice Emerson Bigham, the two greatest reasons that I smile and feel joy. Thank you for letting me read aloud to you and for your patience when I had to spend extra time working through a section of the manuscript or sketching out an idea. My beloved children, as I said in the beginning, this book is for you.